IDENTITY CRISIS

Discovering Your True
Identity in Christ

Evelyn Johnson-Taylor

Also by Evelyn Johnson-Taylor

Seven Blessing Blockers

Identity Crisis by Evelyn Johnson-Taylor
Copyright © 2009 Evelyn Johnson-Taylor

No part of this book may be reproduced, stored in a retrieval system, or transmitted by any means without the permission of the author. Unless otherwise indicated all Scripture quotations are taken from the HOLY BIBLE NEW INTERNATIONAL VERSION ® Copyright © 1973, 1978, 1984 by International Bible Society. Used by permission of Zondervan Publishing House. All rights reserved. Scriptures marked KJV are taken for the King James Version of the Bible. Scripture marked NKJV are taken from the New King James Version of the Bible. Copyright © 1982 by Thomas Nelson, Inc. Used by permission. All rights reserved.

ISBN 978-0-9908338-1-9
For Worldwide Distribution

Promise Publishing House
PO Box 46753
Tampa, FL 33646
info@promisepublishinghouse.com

*This book is dedicated to my husband,
Bishop Scott B. Taylor.
Thank you for your love and support.
Your patience has allowed me to walk
through the different phases of my life
to discover my true purpose.
You have encouraged me to grow and
to develop my walk with God.
Your support has opened the door for me
to be everything God has created me to be.
You are truly God's gift to me!*

Table of Contents

1	The Power of Words	1
2	Who Am I?	11
3	I Am Beautiful	28
4	I Am the Righteousness of God	55
5	I Am Prosperous	73
6	I Am Blessed	90
7	I Am Purpose Driven	105
8	I Am Healed	118
9	I Am Loved	130
10	My True Identity	140

Introduction

Many times we see ourselves as lacking or broken and needing to be fixed. When asked, we can name our shortcomings without any hesitation. On the other hand, if someone said to us, "Tell me something good about yourself," it would be a little more difficult. Why is it that we can easily criticize ourselves, but it is more difficult to applaud ourselves?

One of the reasons we find it challenging to speak excellent words about ourselves is because we do not know who we are. We label ourselves by our surroundings. Our moods are influenced by what is happening in our lives at any given time.

We depend on others to make us happy. The more things we have, the happier we are, or at least that is the way it is supposed to work, right? No, God has empowered us to be all we can be. God has a tremendous plan for our lives.

God has already placed in you everything you need to be all that He has created you to be. Do not look at your current circumstances but focus on the promises of God. Life is a journey, and it takes times to mature and develop.

You may not be where you want to be today, but with God's help, you will accomplish every goal and complete every task in due season. I want to show you through God's Word how you can achieve wholeness and fulfill your destiny. You must make a choice to believe the Word of God.

The sky may seem gray, but the sun will shine again. Hold onto the promises of God because you are who God says you are, and you can do what God said you can do. Always remember, God's Word does not change. The plan God has for you is still good. Learn to listen to God's voice and what He says about who you are.

CHAPTER ONE

The Power of Words

The amount of power that words have on our lives is amazing. The words we use can cause others to have the wrong idea about who we are. Not only can our words influence others, but they can influence how we see ourselves. Many times we speak words from our mouths with no real concept of the power behind them.

When I was a child, my teacher would tell me, "There is no such word as can't." Now I hear young people and adults using that word all the time. The remarkable thing is that if you believe you can't do something, then you will not even try to accomplish the task. On the same note, if you believe you can, then most likely you will be able to not only accomplish the task but excel in your endeavor.

It is no surprise to me that Jesus taught us how important our words are. Read what is recorded in the gospel of Mark:

For verily I say unto you, that whosoever shall say unto this mountain, Be thou removed, and be thou cast into the sea; and shall not doubt in his heart, but shall believe that those things which he saith shall come to pass; he shall have whatsoever he saith (Mark 11:23 KJV).

This scripture does not mean that a man of faith and prayer can be a powerful magician. God acts through us in accordance with His will and not ours. But this scripture does teach us that our faith follows our words. Our faith can be increased by the words we say out of our mouths. The words we use can be liberating or they can be oppressive.

Exercising extreme caution is vital when we are in the presence of negative communication. We must escape the presence of negative talk when at all possible. Monitoring the words we allow to enter through our ears is extremely important. When we listen to negative words over and over, negative thoughts begin to penetrate our hearts.

Be careful what words you use when you describe yourself. Choose your adjectives with care. Our words have great power. The words we choose can be of great encouragement to us or they can be a discouragement to us. The words that we speak over the lives of others can have the same negative or positive effect on them as well.

An accurate description can be a matter of life or death. When a witness to a crime gives the wrong description of the assailant, it causes great turmoil in the lives of those involved. How many people are imprisoned falsely because someone gave the wrong description to the policeman? Many people have spent years behind bars for crimes they did not commit.

To prevent an arrest of the wrong person, the investigating officers search for witnesses who might have seen what happened. These witnesses have to repeat their stories over and over to different people. The law enforcement officers have to prove their story is accurate. Any story that has holes in it will not hold up in court.

Once a mistake has been made in one's identity, it can take years to achieve settlement. Sometimes, after ten and twenty years of false imprisonment, a person is cleared. The charges are dropped, but in many cases the damage is nearly irreversible. Having all the facts before we label anyone is so important.

As damaging as it can be to give the wrong description of someone else, it can be equally damaging when we have the wrong image of ourselves. Although we may not be physically imprisoned, we are imprisoned in our minds. We lock our real potential away, never really discovering our true purpose. We have to be precise in the words we use to depict ourselves. If we use the wrong words when giving an illustration of who we are, we will lead others astray. They will not have a good idea of who we are.

The enemy wants us to believe a story that has holes in it. If we believe the lies of the enemy, we will imprison ourselves. We need to search for the truth of our identity. That truth is found in the Word of God. God is our Creator and He knows who we are.

Identity Crisis

We tell others who we are by the words we say to ourselves and to those around us. We can talk ourselves up, or talk ourselves down. It is very difficult to respect a person who does not respect themselves. When I hear people disrespecting themselves by the words they use to describe themselves, it is very disturbing. In our society today we hear women calling each other vulgar names. Often we see them reacting in an inappropriate way when someone else calls them a vulgar name. You are God's precious jewel. Redefine who you are based on the Word of God.

Many times the key to our success is in our mouths. It is all in what we say to ourselves. We can cause ourselves to succeed or we can cause ourselves to fail. It is crucial what we say to ourselves and equally as vital what we say about ourselves to other people.

What we say to ourselves and what we say about ourselves are very powerful. Have you ever been on a job interview? Do you go in, sit down, and proceed to tell the interviewer all the reasons they should not hire you? No, of course not. You tell them how great you are and how well you can do the job. I have gone on interviews before and speak so positively about myself that I sometimes leave with a confidence I did not have when I walked into the interview. The words we speak have power. In other words, you can talk yourself into believing anything. I know people who talk themselves into believing a lie, and sometimes they can almost talk you into believing it as well.

Some people just will not tell the truth. Lying has

become a part of who they are. They say so many things that are not true that they can no longer make a distinction between fact and fiction. We all know people like that, and we just accept that is who they are. We go on loving and supporting them even though in our hearts we say they will never change.

One of the great things about the Word of God is its power to change people. You may have been caught up in the lies of the enemy, but God's Word has the power to transform your life and show you who you really are.

Frequently I run across people who lie about their age, which seems to be more prevalent among the female gender. But what happens is that after they have lied about their age for so long, they have difficulty remember their correct age.

The problem with lying about your age is that there are many occasions where your correct age is essential. If you have lied about your age for an extended period of time, when the day comes where a correct age is vital, you will have to think awhile before answering. You will have to remember what year you were born and do the math very quickly to be able to give your correct age.

As women, many times we do not want people to know how old we are. It is a major secret, which no one can tell; and if it slips out, we frown upon the tale teller. What is the real purpose of the secret? I believe we lie about our age because the society in which we live places so many expectations on us. If you are a certain age, then you are expected to dress a certain way and already have obtained certain things. We fall into the web of deceitfulness that tells us who we are supposed to be.

Lying about your age can cause problems. For example, when you go in for a physical, you will need to give the physician your correct age. It is very important that the doctor not be misguided during your examination. If the physician is looking at a fifty-year-old body, in order to make an accurate assessment, he needs to know that you are fifty. Your correct age may influence what tests he orders and what medications he prescribes for you.

There are other times when it might not matter if you fluff your responses when asked, "How old are you?" When your preschooler asks you about your age, you might want to fudge a little because you know the first opportunity she is given she will tell the whole class of four year olds her mother's age.

I remember some years ago, when our children were preschoolers, I would laugh under my breath when I would hear kids in my daughter's preschool class say, "My mom is twenty-one." They really believed their moms were twenty-one because that is what the mothers told their children. The interesting thing was that their moms were twenty-one every year. (When moms look good, they can pull off twenty-one for a few years.)

One set of words can talk us into anything, and another set of words can talk us out of anything. We are overcome with fear many times by the words we say to ourselves. Be selective in the words you use when talking about yourself. A true identity is important.

Words are powerful; through them we can make others believe almost anything. With our words we have the ability to convince and influence people. When you have a strong point to make, you choose certain words that affirm your position, words like unquestionably, without a doubt, certainly, definitely, extremely, enormously, and exceptionally, just to name a few.

People who know how to use words stand out in any conversation and have the ability to overshadow everyone in their presence. They are very articulate in their speech. Their pronunciation is faultless. Their diction is magnificent—they always put the right emphasis on the right words. When a person can be very descriptive in their speech, the conversation becomes so much more interesting. People who know how to use words know how powerful words can be.

I have a spiritual daughter like the person I just described. She has the tendency to study people when they speak. She has been known, on occasion, to take notes and critique me when I am speaking. I am thankful that God puts people around us who can help us to better do what He has called us to do. My daughter understands the importance of proper pronunciation and the appropriate use of a word. If our message is to be strong, we have to use the right words in an effective way.

Identity Crisis

Words in Scripture

Let's look at the power of words used in God's holy Word. With many of these scriptures, you will need to read the entire chapter to get the full context. But for our purposes, I just want to show you how affirming words have been used from the beginning of time.

> *Now unto him that is able to do **exceeding abundantly** above all that we ask or think, according to the power that worketh in us* (Ephesians 3:20 KJV, emphasis added).

> *David said, "O LORD, God of Israel, your servant has heard **definitely** that Saul plans to come to Keilah and destroy the town on account of me"* (1 Samuel 23:10, emphasis added).

> *He sent out scouts and learned that Saul had **definitely** arrived* (1 Samuel 26:4, emphasis added).

> *Then Peter came to himself and said, "Now I know **without a doubt** that the Lord sent his angel and rescued me from Herod's clutches and from everything the Jewish people were anticipating"* (Acts 12:11, emphasis added).

> *And **without doubt** the lesser person is blessed by the greater* (Hebrews 7:7, emphasis added).

> *But you must not eat from the tree of the knowledge of good and evil, for when you eat of it you will **surely** die* (Genesis 2:17, emphasis added).

> *I will **surely** bless you and make your descendants as*

numerous as the stars in the sky and as the sand on the seashore. Your descendants will take possession of the cities of their enemies (Genesis 22:17, emphasis added).

*And when the centurion, who stood there in front of Jesus, heard his cry and saw how he died, he said, "**Surely** this man was the Son of God!"* (Mark 15:39, emphasis added).

*Four things on earth are small, yet they are **extremely** wise* (Proverbs 30:24, emphasis added).

*I was advancing in Judaism beyond many Jews of my own age and was **extremely** zealous for the traditions of my fathers* (Galatians 1:14, emphasis added).

These are just a few scriptures in the Bible that use strong words. There are many others. What I want us to see is that words are used to stress points, even in scripture. When we hear and read words like the ones pointed out above, we are more prone to believe them. The strength of the words used in a sentence makes the statement more or less powerful. It is imperative that we be watchful of the words we speak out of our mouths. We need to also be careful of the words that we entertain in our heart after they enter through our ears.

The tongue has the power of life and death and those who love it will eat its fruit (Proverbs 18:21 NKJV).

Even so the tongue is a little member and boasts great things. See how great a forest a little fire kindles! And the tongue is a fire, a world of iniquity. The tongue is so set among our members that it defiles the whole body and sets on fire the course of nature; and it is set on fire by hell (James 3:5-6 NKJV).

The words you say yield great power. An uncontrolled tongue can defile the whole body. If we fail to control our tongue, we have a problem as deep as sin.

What are you saying about yourself? What are you calling yourself? Are you identifying yourself correctly, or do you have a mistaken identity? How do we know what the right description is? Is it how my parents described me? Is it what people around me say?

Your true identity is found in the Word of God. You are who God says you are, and you can do what God says you can do.

CHAPTER TWO

Who Am I?

Many of us go through years of our lives searching for purpose. It is the deepest desire of every person to discover their true identity. As young children our parents called us sweet names such as precious, darling, baby, or sweetie. In Mom and Dad's ears, every word that comes out of our mouth is precious.

When we have young children, many of us keep the video camera on the tripod so it will always be ready and in the record mode. We want to capture every moment. Even now when our family goes back and reviews the tapes, it warms my heart that we have such precious memories.

As parents we do not want to miss a moment of our baby's words, and we want to share our delight with everyone we know. Every conversation, no matter how it starts, ends with us talking about our little ones. Parents can talk about their children for hours and hours and never get bored. Others may get bored from listening, but we continue to talk. No story is too private, and no story is too long in the eyes of a parent.

As a single woman, I worked as a registered nurse at Capitol Hill Hospital in Washington, D.C. Around the lunch table in the cafeteria, every conversation with other intensive care nurses would be about their children. It never bothered me to listen because I understood how much mothers enjoy talking about their children. In fact, I would schedule myself to work every Christmas so a mom could have time off with her children.

One nurse whom I remember very well would always apologize for talking so much about her children. I was not sure why she was apologizing, but I later understood. I would hear my single coworkers saying things like, "Why do they always talk about their kids?" or "No one wants to hear about your kids all the time." Some people do have a problem with others talking about their children all the time. (Of course, the individuals who mind usually are those who have never experienced the joy of listening to the little voice of their own child.)

Children tend to have the most sincere opinions about life. They tell it just like it is with no beating around the bush. No wonder Jesus said we should come as little children to Him. Our motives must be sincere. We cannot come seeking what we can gain, but we should come desiring to be used by our Lord and Savior Jesus Christ.

Who Am I?

Children exhibit sincerity, enthusiasm, and a completely naive attitude. They rely totally on their parents. Therefore, childlikeness is an appropriate example for the qualities a follower of Christ should have.

I tell you the truth, anyone who will not receive the kingdom of God like a little child will never enter it (Mark 10:15).

As our children grow and are introduced to others of influence, they learn more about who they are. In school the teacher may describe them one way while their classmates may give an entirely different opinion. The teacher may consider a student who is attentive to be a good student. A classmate may consider that same student to be brown-nosing and call them the teacher's pet. When you are a child, your friends can be very cruel with their words at times.

As teens, our identity becomes a major issue in our lives and we scream, "Who am I?" By the time we reach adulthood, we think we have it all resolved. We have made it through puberty, and we are now ready for our autonomy, or so we think. Are we really equipped for the world? Do we really know what we want and where we are headed? In other words, do you know who you are?

Many times we shy away from our true identity because we are not ready to accept who we are. Some of us live in denial, not wanting to accept our true identity. The same way we talk ourselves into things, we can talk ourselves out of things. My parents may tell me that I have great potential and can do anything I set my mind to, but because I am afraid of failing, I speak the opposite to myself. I tell myself I cannot do it because I am not capable, and so I do not try.

When I tell myself enough times I cannot do something, I start to believe I cannot do it. Because I do not believe I can do it, I will not try very hard if at all. If I do not try, then I am right—I cannot do it. So I bypass an opportunity to discover my potential.

Yet the journey continues for me to discover my true identity. I investigate and explore, not really knowing where to look, but looking nevertheless. Just when we think we have a sense of direction as to where we are going, things become complicated.

It seems that in early adulthood the questions are in actuality just beginning. As we embark on our journey to claim our place in the world, it can be very bewildering. How can I declare my spot if I am uncertain of who I am? What do I want to be when I grow up? Can I be what I want to be, or do I have to be what others want me to be? How can I be true to myself? Authenticity is the cry of our hearts. I just want to be me. But how can I be me if I do not know who I am?

When the time comes for me to seek employment, I am presented with a new set of challenges. If I do not know who I am, then how will I know what kind of further schooling to obtain or employment to seek? Society will try to dictate to us who we are and what we are supposed to be doing.

Who Am I?

Just because we become an adult does not mean we have left the halls of peer pressure. We are bombarded with pressure from every side to be something we are not. For example, we are influenced by the media and its advertisements, telling us how we should dress. Information comes at us from all sides; some of it is good and some of it not so good.

External pressures force us to walk with a certain stride to demonstrate our confidence so others will know we are important people. There is so much for us to live up to, but it is complex if we still do not know who we are. Directions are coming at us from every angle—to whom do we listen? What do we disregard? What happens if we obtain the wrong information and disregard the correct information? We have so many questions that need answers. If only we knew where to go to get the answers we need.

While growing up, we have heard many voices telling us who we are. Many of them are pessimistic. These unenthusiastic words spoken from those who have the power to influence our destiny can be extremely damaging. Whether the words are from a parent or someone else we respect, negative words can be detrimental. People we love and respect will sometimes speak words over us with no idea how they will impact our growth and maturity. Often the person speaking negative words does not realize the power of those words. But more importantly, the person to whom the depressing words have been spoken does not realize the harm that is being done as he or she receives them.

We have to be careful what comes out of our mouths.

Many times we would like to take our words back, but once the words have gone out, they cannot be retrieved. The same principle applies when we speak negatively about ourselves. The words we speak go into the atmosphere, and it starts the cycle of negative thinking.

There was a spiritually mature woman in the church I attended as a young adult. She would often say to me regarding my singleness, "What are you waiting for? When are you going to get married? You are not getting any younger." I felt she should have been encouraging me to seek God for a mate and tell me to be willing to wait for the right one. She was someone I respected, and I was looking to receive encouragement and a sense of who I was from her. Instead, she would say other things to me that caused me to doubt who I was. She probably did not realize how such destructive statements could have pressured me to marry the wrong person.

I am grateful to God that even in those years I understood that I should not receive destructive words into my spirit. This was a woman I admired, but I could not allow the words she spoke to impact my decisions in a negative way. Many times we let others pressure us into doing things we would not normally do just by the words they say to us.

I daily use one of the lessons I learned in the midst of this. I encourage single women to seek God for a mate. I teach them not to let age be a factor in their decision making. God's timing is perfect, although it may seem late to us. My mother used to tell us that God is always on time. He may not come when you want Him, but He is on time. My experience has been He is not usually early, but He is never late.

Occasionally a teacher will unwisely call a student names such as stupid, crazy, retarded, or dumb. Powerful adults sometimes call impressionable kids names that are not a true descriptions of who they really are. They might make a statement such as, "You are stupid! You will never accomplish anything! You are a loser," just to name a few. These are statements of death to a child. Many times others have already decided what we will be, what we will become, and what we will accomplish, and are sure to tell us of their judgment.

When the prophet Samuel went to anoint the next king, David was missing from the lineup. Jesse had all of his sons parade in front of the prophet Samuel except David. The Lord said He had not chosen any of them. Samuel asked Jesse if he had another son. Jesse responded, "Yes, but he is tending the sheep." Samuel said, "Send for him, and we will not sit down until he comes." David's family had already decided he was going to be a shepherd so he was not included when his brothers were presented to the prophet Samuel as the next potential king. (For the full story, read 1 Samuel 16.)

Many times others have already told us who we will be, but God has other plans. People put limits on us by the way they speak. They will say words that will cause us to doubt who we are. Their words will occasionally cause us to sit back and not even try. You must remember that your fate is not in the hands of man, but God decides who we are. If you want to know who you are, check out the Word of God for a true description.

People will try to doom us with their words. Whoever says, "Sticks and stones may break my bones, but words will never hurt me," obviously does not realize the power of their words. Anyone who has ever had negative words spoken over their life knows that sticks and stones are not the only thing that hurt—words injure also. The pain from sticks and stones are temporary. The pain from words can present someone with a lifelong challenge to overcome the emotional harm that has been done.

I minister to many women who suffer from low self-esteem. When I counsel with them, our conversations almost always go back to a time when they were a young girl and were violated in some way. The violation is usually some form of abuse, many times verbal. Perhaps someone told them as a young girl that they would never amount to anything, or someone made them feel as if they were not good enough. Many of the women I speak to were criticized as children, and they grew up to form relationships with critical people. They marry men who are cruel and critical; as a result, the women continue to have an identity crisis.

For every depressing name you have been called, it will take many encouraging words spoken to you to combat the negative effect. If you have been called ugly all your life, it will take more than one person telling you that you are beautiful in order for you to believe it. I have heard people say,

Who Am I?

"No one listens to me." That is not true; someone is always listening to you. Whether you know it or not, some people believe what you say, so be careful what you say.

One of the interesting things about people is that they are more prone to believe you when you do not want them to do so. In other words, when you are just joking around, someone will take your words as the truth. Words can kill our influence and hurt our authority.

People have been swayed in a different direction because of what they hear someone say about someone else. Many times there is nothing to support the words, but someone believed them without requiring any proof. Ministries have been harmed because of negative words spoken about the leaders. Pastors have lost their credibility because someone spoke out of turn. Someone will always believe what they hear, whether it is true or not. We really have to be careful of what comes out of our mouths.

When our children were young, we had to be very careful that we did not speak negatively about anyone in front of them. If you say something in front of young children, you never know when or where they will repeat it. That is why I am not shocked today when I teach in the middle schools and hear children using all kinds of foul language. Oftentimes it is a direct reflection on what is being said in their homes. This is not always true, but more often than not children learn what they live.

Many times we adopt the philosophy, "Do as I say, not as

I do." That may seem to get us off the hook, but this is not a good way to relate to our children. They always do what they see us do anyway. They say what they hear us say without fail. They tend to pick up our most undesirable habits. It would be amusing if they only picked up our good habits, but life does not work that way. It would appear that our children inherit our most undesirable qualities.

The same way they pick up our negative qualities, they pick up our negative attitudes. If you have a bad attitude, others around you will be touched by it. Our attitude reflects the words that come out of our mouths. If our attitude is terrible, then the words that we speak will not be inspirational to others.

I was convinced that my infants could tell when I was not feeling good. I think they could sense my negative vibrations and be more restless than usual. This always causes frustration because when you are not feeling good is when you need the baby to behave nicely. In my experience my babies acted the way I felt. Our attitude can create either a nurturing environment or a stressful one.

The Scripture teaches us:

Death and life are in the power of the tongue, And those who love it will eat its fruit (Proverbs 18:21).

When statements are made by someone in authority, the simplest words take on new meaning. Not only can words be damaging, but it also makes a difference out of whose mouth the words came. In grade school a buddy may call you stupid and you can receive it as a funny joke, but it is by no means funny when a teacher or parent refers to you in that way.

When you have been told again and again that you are no good and will never amount to anything, you develop a case of mistaken identity. You assume the identity of the label that has been placed on you. You begin to act stupid and do unintelligent things. We sometimes sabotage ourselves simply because we believe what someone else has said about us. The words take on lives of their own, and we find ourselves living up to the words that have been spoken about us.

The good news is that this works both ways. We can strive to live up to the constructive things that have been said about us as well. We can choose what we want to listen to and what we want to receive. Are you familiar with the phase, "Garbage in, garbage out?" In other words, be careful what words you receive. Watch what you allow to penetrate your heart. Whatever goes into the heart is what comes out of the heart. The scripture says it this way:

For as he thinketh in his heart, so is he (Proverbs 23:7 KJV).

But the things that come out of the mouth come from the heart, and these make a man "unclean" **(**Matthew 15:18**).**

But those things which proceed out of the mouth come forth from the heart; and they defile the man (Matthew 15:18 KJV).

O generation of vipers, how can ye, being evil, speaks good things? for out of the abundance of the heart the mouth speaketh (Matthew 12:34 KJV).

The next time negative words come out of your mouth, you should check your heart. Our speech is a reflection of what we have in our hearts. People do not know what is in our hearts until we speak. That is one of the reasons it is so important that we speak into the lives of our children. They need to know that we are proud of them. A child needs to hear their parent's approval from the lips of the parent. Never leave it up to them to figure out who they are—you have to tell them.

Instead of a daddy telling his little girl how she is always messing up, he can tell her how beautiful she is. Instead of telling her how she cannot do something, he should be encouraging her that she can. In some cases a dad says nothing, and then the child is left to decide his or her own identity.

Silence can be as damaging as negative words. It is the role of the father to speak into the lives of his children. The father has to announce to his children who they are and what they can accomplish. It is the father's role to give his son or daughter an identity. The father must proclaim in the life of his children who they are and help them to discover their purpose. Our children will have many voices speaking in their ears. It is the responsibility of the parents to be the loudest voice of them all.

For every person who tells your children that they will not

succeed, you have to tell them over and over that they will indeed succeed. For every person who tells your children that they will fail, you must affirm to them over and over that they will succeed so that they will persevere.

I can do everything through him who gives me strength (Philippians 4:13).

We have to teach God's Word to our children. We have to let them know that with God's help they can accomplish anything.

"If you can?" said Jesus. "Everything is possible for him who believes" (Mark 9:23).

The way you teach your children to have faith is by demonstrating faith to them. Let them see you believing and trusting God. The Scripture teaches us in James 2:18-26 that our faith is no good if we have no deeds to show for it. These verses in James give us examples of those who let their faith work for them. In fact, the writer says that faith without deeds is dead. When our children see our faith in action, their faith will grow.

Many times children want to do everything they see their parents do. When we demonstrate our faith to our children, they will want to be like us in that way too.

In Proverbs Solomon teaches us about our role in teaching our children. (Read the entire Proverbs as this theme is woven throughout that book.) It is our duty; we cannot leave it up to the childcare providers. Many times we send our kids to school, wanting the teacher to straighten them out. It is not the teacher's job to parent our children. It is our responsible to train them up in the ways of the Lord.

When we send them out of our houses, they need to have our character. The temperament they show the world is the one we have demonstrated for them according to God's Word. If they know who they are when they go out into the world, they are less likely to display a counterfeit personality and be persuaded by what the devil has to offer them.

More than thirty years ago, I was in nursing school, and math was presenting an enormous challenge for me. I contemplated giving up and quitting nursing school. I remember my father coming into my bedroom and saying to me, "Remember who you are; you can do this." I often wonder if he knew what impact those words would have on me. He was affirming to me who I was and what I could do.

Not many days later, a light bulb came on in my head and I understood math. Not only did I understand it, but I was able to tutor my classmates in it. Parents, your words are powerful, that is why it is so important to make sure you are saying the right words to your children.

If my father had said, "You're right; you will never be able to understand math," my life would have certainly taken a different path. Just as I remember his positive words many years later, I would have remembered them if they had been negative. I would have become a product of my environment. I would have gone on to pass the same negative reinforcement to my children. Parents, our words have long-range and

Who Am I?

long-term affects, not only with our children but in generations to come.

Perhaps you did not have an earthly father to remind you of your true identity. Maybe someone spoke false statements to you, and you grew up with a mistaken identity. You think that you cannot do what you are called to do. You think that you are a failure and will never amount to anything. I want to introduce you to the truth of God's Word.

You are who God says you are, and you can do what God says you can do. Your heavenly Father wants to confirm your identity today. After years of listening to the wrong voices, you think that you are somebody that you are not. God wants to tell you who you really are. He wants to show you through the truth of His Word.

It does not matter what other have said about you. It does not matter how you start out; what counts is where you end up. What God has to say about you is the deciding factor. Make the decision today to let God be the final word in determining your true identity. Choose to believe what God has said about you. His Word and His Word alone is the final authority.

Many times in my life when I have heard negative things, I went back to God's Word. When I hear people say, "You will not be able to accomplish that," I go back to the Word of God and read:

I can do everything through him who gives me strength (Philippians 4:13).

Identity Crisis

    I want to teach you how you can be everything that God said you can be. You are not a loser; you are a winner. You are not a failure; you are a success. My prayer is that you understand that you can do everything that God said you can do. Not only can you do what He said you can do, but you can be who He created you to be. God really does have the last word regarding your true identity.

Let us pray.

Dear Heavenly Father,

From time to time I am confused about my identity. I remember the negative words that have been spoken over me. Even as a child when I was told I would never amount to anything, I remember thinking if Mom and Dad do not believe in me, then maybe I will never amount to anything. Because of Your Word, I now know that I can, according to Scripture, do all things through Christ who gives me the strength. I give my insecurities to You today. I release myself of the labels that have been put on me by others. Heavenly Father, I receive Your Word and what You have to say about me. I thank You in Jesus' name. Amen.

CHAPTER THREE

I Am Beautiful

It has been often said that beauty is in the eye of the beholder. You can love someone, live in the same house with them, and still have a different eye when it comes to beauty. No two people see everything alike.

In marriages many couples have a different opinion on what is beautiful. Because of this difference, home decorating can become a major issue. If a couple cannot agree on the decorations, usually one person will back down and give complete control to the other person. Sometimes the person relinquishing control will use it as a bargaining chip later.

In other words, you may get control of decorating the home, but do not expect to have 100 percent control of the landscaping too. When we built our home, my husband asked for one room to decorate precisely the way he wanted it. Who could turn down an offer like that? I was able to choose the decoration for the entire house except that one room. Concessions sometimes have to be made to live peacefully in the beautifully decorated home.

When we call a person beautiful, we are looking at both the inner beauty, which may include personality and intelligence, and the outer beauty. When we look at the outer beauty, we look at things like health, body type, skin tone, and condition of the hair. We look at the height and weight and whether are not it is proportional.

Outer beauty is dependent upon who is doing the looking. That is one of the reason beauty pageants in my opinion are so controversial and dangerous. We base the winners on the opinions of the judges. Inner beauty, on the other hand, is more difficult to quantify, though beauty pageants claim to take this into consideration as well. How can one know what is in the heart of another person? Only God knows the heart of man.

I strongly believe that beauty is in the eye of the beholder. You can be sitting next to a person and both look at the same object but see it in a totally different light. The "beauty is in the eyes of the beholder" phrase means that something or someone is beautiful, depending on who is doing the looking.

Somebody said one man's treasure is another man's junk. What one person puts out with the trash may be valuable to someone else. That is why yard sales and flea markets are so successful. We all know that just because we do not want something anymore, it does not mean no one else wants it.

Identity Crisis

Knowing others can use what we no longer find useful forces us to save the goods and wait for a garage sale day, knowing we can redeem some of the purchase cost for these items we cannot use anymore.

I have never been a good yard sale shopper. You have to be able to visualize potential in order to shop at yard sales. When I shop, I need the display and all the trimmings around the items I purchase. I know people who go to yard sales, buy an object, and use it for something totally different than its intended purpose. The people who can do that are people with vision.

There are visionaries and there are people like me who need to see the finished product. My husband is the visionary of our home, thank God. Even though I am not a visionary at yard sales, it does not stop me from selling things there. My husband, on the other hand, can look at a piece and see value in it. He would make a good yard sale shopper. Though we are creatively different, we complement each other well.

Everyone is uniquely created; no two people are exactly alike. One can be birthed from the same mother and father and be very different. I have two daughters, and believe me when I say just because you have the same parents does not mean you are similar. Two can have the same nurturing, grow up in the same environment, and yet be as different from one another as night is from day.

Even identical twins do not necessarily enjoy the same foods or same activities. They may look alike, but many times that is where the similarities end. Often they will have totally different mannerisms. One will be quiet and the other one thunderous. Twins sometime will have the same hair color but a different texture of hair. Another physical difference between identical twins is their fingerprints. The fingerprint is similar but they are not exactly the same.

Studies have shown that identical twins may have similar marks when they are born. But, as they age, the marks in their DNA become more and more different. Even though identical twins have the same DNA, the DNA is used in a different way. Identical twins can be different in height and size. Many times one is born weighing more than the other. One thing that seems to be the same is that identical twins almost always have the same eye color. But even with the same eye color, they do not always see the beauty the other one sees.

How many times have we commented on our young children's artwork, "Honey, that's beautiful," but if we had to tell someone what the drawing was, we would have no idea. We stare at the drawings, hoping for a clue as to what we are looking at. We pray for a hint as to what the drawings are, not wanting to call them the wrong thing. We just tell them that it is beautiful because it does not matter what it is supposed to be. The drawing is beautiful simply because our beautiful child colored it. If a loving parent is doing the looking, it does not matter what the drawing is supposed to be. In the eyes of the parent, it is a beautiful drawing. On the other hand, a stranger might look at the same picture and not see what the parents have seen. When I think about some of the things our children have given us over the years, many of them we could not identify. I have to say beauty is in the eye of the beholder.

Beauty is not just an eye thing; it is also a heart thing. When we as parents look at the project our child has so proudly displayed, we look with the heart and not just with the eye. Our eyes alone would say, "What in the world is that?" but our hearts would say, "I love it." Many of you know what I am talking about firsthand.

If you have never had this experience, wait and your turn will come. The day will come when you mistake a drawing of a giraffe for a tree. As a parent you will learn that everything has to be displayed. When we flaunt these items, we are affirming to our children that they have value. What you are saying is that the picture they have colored has significance to you because they are precious to you.

Displaying a drawing is affirming the worth of the child as well as the merit of the painting. Even as I write this I am smiling, thinking about our Christmas tree and the ornament that we still so proudly display from the "What is it?" pile. Many of them we still have not been able to name, but we display them every year. The only thing we know for sure is that our precious children created them with their loving hands. In the eyes of loving parents, this is enough to call something beautiful.

I love nice paintings and colorful artwork. We have several prized possessions that adorn the walls of our home.

Most, if not all of them, I had assistance in selecting. I do not know much about art, but I know what I like when I see it.

Because of my limited knowledge regarding this subject, I am smart to solicit the help of others. I have to rely on the knowledge of experts to tell me if what I like is worth its price tag. Sometimes it may not be worth the ticket price, but can you really put a value on what brings you pleasure?

My limited knowledge of art would possibly cause me to overlook a priceless piece. It could also cause me to invest in a worthless piece as well. That is why it is important to let others help you in areas where you lack understanding. I lack understanding when it comes to selecting pieces of artwork. I rely on someone with an understanding of art to tell me what a fine piece of art is and what is not. Notice, I rely on someone with an understanding, not just anyone.

When we do not know who we are, we have to rely on God's Word to tell us who we are and who we are not. We cannot take everything someone says to us and receive it. We need to ask, "What does the expert say? What does God say?"

Beauty is indeed in the eye of the beholder. True beauty is not always seen on the exterior. In fact, the exterior can be very deceiving as to what is really in the heart of a person. Genuine beauty is more than what we see on the outside. In order to be able to discern real beauty, you have to know something about the subject.

To be proficient in choosing a beautiful and valuable

Identity Crisis

painting, you have to know something about art. You have to know the names of artists. You have to know a little history on the artist and what his creative style is. Then you will know what symbols to look for in order to make a distinction between a fake piece of artwork and an authentic one.

If you do not feel equipped to select genuine pieces of artwork on your own, you will need someone who has a working knowledge of art to assist you. In other words, we have to look deeper than what we see with our natural eye.

If you want to know if someone is truly beautiful, you must know something about the person. You will need to know more than what appears before your eyes. Many times we take things at face value. When you only take what you see on the surface, you can often make a costly mistake.

Many times precious gems are overlooked because on the exterior they do not appear precious. But when you take the time to research the matter, you may discover something very valuable inside. Often the gem has to be looked at under a microscope to determine its true value by a certified gemologist specializing in jewelry. However, I have read that if you run across a ring at a yard sale, there are certain things you can look for to learn if it is valuable.

For example, if it is a diamond, hold it up to the sunlight and see if the stone refracts light. Diamonds refract so much light. One other thing I heard (but do not try this and blame me if it does not work), is that if you shine a small light through the stone and cannot see it on the other side but only a bright halo around the rim, it is more likely to be a true diamond. My disclaimer to this information is that these are things I have heard over the years. But my point is that to accurately identify a real diamond you have to consult an expert.

Many people may want to speak into your life and tell you who you are. The truth of the matter is that if you want to know who you really are, you need to go to the expert. The Word of God is the final authority on who you are.

With knowledge comes power and the ability to make an informed decision. You need a working knowledge of the subject you are observing. The Scripture teaches:

Get wisdom, get understanding; do not forget my words or swerve from them (Proverbs 4:5).

Wisdom is supreme; therefore get wisdom. Though it cost all you have, get understanding (Proverbs 4:7).

How much better to get wisdom than gold, to choose understanding rather than silver! (Proverbs 16:16).

He who gets wisdom loves his own soul; he who cherishes understanding prospers (Proverbs 19:8).

Buy the truth and do not sell it; get wisdom, discipline and understanding (Proverbs 23:23).

With the proper knowledge you can deem something beautiful or not so beautiful. When you know what causes a person to be beautiful, you know what to look for. Too often we label others based on what we see. We must search deeper to understand the true identity of a person.

We must learn to see others, as well as ourselves, through the eyes of our Creator. The Word of God is our mirror to show us precisely who we are. Trust the expert; God made us and since He is the Creator, I am sure He knows indisputably who we are.

My people are destroyed for lack of knowledge. Because you have rejected knowledge, I also will reject you from being my priest. Since you have forgotten the law of Your God, I also will forget your children (Hosea 4:6 KJV).

If we want to know real beauty, we need the knowledge of God. If I want to know if I am beautiful or not, I do not ask designers or fashion experts. What looks beautiful to one may or may not look beautiful to another.

Just look at the various fashion designers. One of the reasons we have so many of them who are able to thrive in their businesses is because everyone has a different taste. If we all liked the same thing, then there would be no need for various designers. We would only need one designer to satisfy everyone. Because we all have our individual ideas of what is beautiful and what is not, we need different designers to fulfill our diverse likes and dislikes. Our sense of style and taste is unique.

We see our individuality exhibited every day. The next time you are out driving, take a look around at all the different models of automobiles. How many times have you

I Am Beautiful

looked at a car and said, "That is an ugly car." I know I do it often. But the reality is that I am not driving that car and the person who is, more than likely thinks it is an appealing car. More importantly if I am not paying for the car, what does it matter to me anyway. But that is just the way we are—we like to offer our opinions. Many times we are quick to offer an opinion when the other person exhibits interests different from ours. We often want others to be fond of what we like and to perform as we do.

Look in your neighborhood and see the different styles of homes. We choose one builder over the other because we like the style of the homes they build. Some builders have a reputation of maximizing the space, while others have a reputation of wasting space.

When we were building a home, I wanted a linen closet in the master bedroom, but the builder did not want to put one there. The builder gave me all the reasons why it would not be feasible to make that adjustment to the plans.

We had what I identified as wasted space because a linen closet could have very easily gone in at the end of the hall leading to the master bedroom. Saying it was not practical was more than likely the builder's way of not wanting to change the architectural plans. In other words, that builder would not be my choice for another building project. Now, I am sure somebody else loves the way that builder works; otherwise he would not still be in business. My point is we all have different likes and dislikes. We are created unique; no two individuals are exactly alike.

Our various likes and dislikes are seen in the way we decorate our homes. Some people think wallpaper is beautiful while others detest it. Still others like paneling on the walls of their home. Thank God for diversity; our world would be very monotonous if everyone had the same tastes.

Even restaurants would have to go out of business if everyone had the same taste in foods. Can you image everyone eating the same kind of food? I can hear my daughter say, "How can anyone like vegetables?" Grocery stores would have to close if they did not carry the one food everyone was eating. Ask yourself, "What would the world be like if everyone was just like me?"

When we talk about beauty and where our real beauty lies, we must look beyond what the mirror on the wall shows us. If I want to know if I am beautiful or not, I must go back to the first One who knew me. Who was the first one to behold my beauty? Not my mom or my dad. Who was the first person to behold me? Who knew me before anyone else knew me? The scripture records in Jeremiah 1:5,

> *Before I formed you in the womb I knew you, before you were born I set you apart; I appointed you as a prophet to the nations.*

I believe the same God who knew Jeremiah, knew you and He knew me. God knew you first. Before the foundation of the world He had you in mind. You were destined to be here. Your mom and dad may have thought they were planning a pregnancy, but God had already established the plan.

You were not a mistake, even though you might have snuck up on your parents. God knew you were coming even if your mom thought she was finished having babies and you were a surprise. My friend, you were not a surprise to God. He was expecting you, and you arrived right on time. Nothing is a surprise to God. Our heavenly Father makes no mistakes. Everything is timed and purpose oriented.

The Bible says that God created us in His image.

So God created man in his own image, in the image of God he created him; male and female he created them (Genesis 1:27).

The Scripture also records that everything God made was good. (Read Genesis 1.) Since I was created by God and He called everything He created good, then I am good. When I know my Creator, it gives me a deeper insight into who I really am. I understand that I was created by the hands of a loving God.

The truth of the matter is that if I am to know my real beauty, I must know my origin. I have to know my beginning, starting point, cause, or ultimate source from which I derived. Yes, although Mom and Dad are the delivery people, God is the ultimate source. I have to know where I came from to know who I really am.

Once I have a relationship with my Creator, I can make an informed decision about who I really am. When I know the Designer personally, then I know who I am. When I spend quality time with the One who made me, He tells me everything I need to know about me.

I do not need to depend on society to tell me who I am. Neither do I depend on commercial ads or my peers to give me an identity. My Creator has already told me who I am. I will not have an identity crisis because I know who I am. I will not freak out because not only do I know who I am, but I also know whose I am. I will give thanks to God for whom He made me to be. I will praise Him because I am beautiful.

I praise you because I am fearfully and wonderfully made; your works are wonderful, I know that full well (Psalms 139:14).

God made me exceptional; there is no one before me like me nor will there be anyone after me just like me. I was created beautiful by the hands of my loving Creator. When I look at myself in the mirror I see a rare edition.

My external features may favor a certain family member, but the part of me that makes me unique is my spirit. I am beautiful and so are you. No matter how many people tell me I look like my mother, or I act like my father, I am my own person. I have my parents' DNA of course, but I am not a duplicate of anyone. God made only one of me. Somebody said, "When God made you, He broke the mold." In other words, there will never be another you.

It is vital that you have a working knowledge of God's Word if you are going to know your true identity. Knowledge is acquired only by the use of your own mind in study. We must study God's Word to discover our true identity.

But grow in the grace and knowledge of our Lord and Savior Jesus Christ (2 Peter 3:18).

Study to shew thyself approved unto God, a workman that needeth not to be ashamed, rightly dividing the word of truth (2 Timothy 2:15 KJV).

When we study the Word of God, we will know what His Word says about us.

*He has made everything **beautiful** in its time. He has also set eternity in the hearts of men; yet they cannot fathom what God has done from beginning to end* (Ecclesiastes 3:11, emphasis added).

Our lives may not turn out as we had hoped, but that does not take anything away from the way God made us. Do not let anyone tell you that you are not beautiful. You are exactly the way God made you on purpose. I have heard others say, "God does not make junk." Everything God does is good, and He does not make mistakes.

Do not be fooled by the labels put on you by other people. You are God's original. He knows who you are, and He is first and foremost concerned about the condition of your heart. Man looks on the outward appearance, but God looks at the heart.

In Scripture being only outward beautiful is compared to

being whitewashed tombs. Looking beautiful on the outside can be very deceiving regarding what is on the inside.

> *Woe to you, teachers of the law and Pharisees, you hypocrites! You are like whitewashed tombs, which look* **beautiful** *on the outside but on the inside are full of dead men's bones and everything unclean* (Matthew 23:27, emphasis added).

We may clean up nicely, but if no transformation has taken place in our heart, we are not pleasing to God.

We must teach our young children that inner beauty is more important than expensive clothes, makeup, and jewelry. We can get weekly manicures and pedicures, but it is our hearts that love God. Our hearts are what demonstrates our true beauty. God is more concerned with the state of our hearts than the status of our wardrobes.

It concerns me greatly that we as a people invest so much time and energy in our external features. We sometimes spend more time in the mirror looking for spots and wrinkles than we do on our knees confessing our faults. God has the final say on who we are and on whom we will become. Our Creator created us for His glory, and we are beautiful to Him.

The prophet Samuel was sent to anoint the next king after Saul. The mistake that he made was that he was looking for someone who looked like he could be king. He was looking for someone who looked the part—muscular, tall, strong, and with a perfect physique. But God had someone else in mind.

I Am Beautiful

But the Lord said to Samuel, "Do not consider his appearance or his height, for I have rejected him. The LORD does not look at the things man looks at. Man looks at the outward appearance, but the LORD looks at the heart" (1 Samuel 16:7).

I do not know about you, but I am so glad God looks at my heart. Sometimes I do not look like a Christian or even feel like a Christian. But I am so thankful that my eternal life is not based on how I look or feel. It is based on the fact that I have received Jesus Christ by faith into my heart.

I have committed my life to striving every day to obey His Word. So if you just looked at me, you might miss who I really am. You cannot look at a person's exterior and determine his or her relationship with God. I am so glad that when we do not feel the part, God sees our heart. Beloved, God is looking at your heart. He sees the beauty in you.

I have two teenage daughters, and I pray for them daily because I know how society has put so much emphasis on our external beauty. We are constantly pressured by the world's standards. The yardstick by which the world measures beauty is flawed at best. The many voices we hear in the media are messing with the minds of our children, causing many of them to struggle with their identity. They walk around confused, trying to measure up to an unattainable standard.

If the system is broken, and it is, whoever compares themselves using the broken system will get a false result. When we measure ourselves by the world's standards, we

Identity Crisis

have a false identity. We are identifying ourselves using incorrect information.

Many times our children are led to believe that their identity is based on what kind of shoes they wear. How ludicrous! They are unfairly judged by how big of an allowance they receive and other silly things that have no real significance to their true identity. Not only do our children feel pressure from their peers but also sometimes right from within their own homes.

Our children feel pressured to have the most recent and the greatest styles of everything in order to fit in with their peers. They are made to feel like they do not measure up unless they have what others have. Our society has sold us a false identity, and we have bought into it hook, line, and sinker.

Mom and Dad sometimes have unrealistic expectations. We pressure our children to conform to their peers. One of the ways we do this is by trying to keep up with the Joneses. If my neighbor buys her daughter a designer bag, then I must buy my daughter one also. What are we teaching our children?

When we shop, we search to see whose name is on our clothes and in the clothes we buy for our children. (I am talking about clothes with the expensive designers' labels.) We do these things in the name of making ourselves beautiful.

Why are we doing these things? Many times we do it to

impress those around us. We want to be beautiful in the eyes of others. What about being beautiful in the eyes of the One who made you? What about beautifying your heart and nurturing it the way we nurture our physical bodies? Please do not get me wrong; I am not at all against taking care of the body. I do martial arts three days a week and cardiovascular workouts in between, but the Scripture does say:

> *What good will it be for a man if he gains the whole world, yet forfeits his soul? Or what can a man give in exchange for his soul?* (Matthew 16:26).

In other words, nothing is as important as our souls. According to *Merriam-Webster's Dictionary*, our soul is the immaterial essence of our lives—the spiritual entity in each of us. We must guard our souls. Nothing is of more value than a sincere soul. No matter how much you have, material things will not satisfy the longings of the soul.

I am sometimes stunned when I go to my daughter's high school and see the kind of cars parked in the students' parking lot. Some of them might be parents' cars, but I have it on good authority that some of them are students' vehicles. These are students with no jobs. Some of the cars were purchased by the parents before the students knew how to drive. I have to question what are we teaching our children. Are we teaching them about who they are from the inside, or are we teaching them that the one with the most toys wins? Imparting truth into our children is critical. We have been commissioned by God to train and teach them.

We need to tell them the real meaning of joy and happiness. They need to know that real beauty is on the inside, and real success comes from knowing Jesus and having a relationship with Him. Our children need to see us seeking after the things of God and not the materialistic things of the world.

I am not opposed to people having nice things. However, I am in opposition to material things replacing our real value. I frequently tell my daughters to look past what they see on the outside of a person. As human beings we can only see the external expression of a person. Often that is a mask they use to hide the true identity of who they are.

One of my teenage daughters will say things like, "Mom, he is so cute." I respond by saying, "You know nothing about him; you do not even know if he can read." Then I follow up by asking, "Does he know Jesus?" She will respond, "He is still cute." But my point is that the exterior is a very small part of who we are. Many potential good friendships are never birthed because we focus on what people look like on the outside.

When my children are involved in a conflict with a peer, I encourage them to look at the whole person. What is the child's home life like? What kind of relationship do they have with their parents? Do they get enough attention? What else is that child dealing with? Many times children will act out because of lack of attention. I want my children to get to know the real person and not judge others by what they see on the exterior.

One thing I have experienced working with children is that many of them appear hard on the exterior, but deep down they are really very sweet. After all they are still children, and children need love and attention to do well.

What is perhaps aggravating to you may be that person's way of asking, "Will you be my friend?" I do not want my daughters building relationships with people because of what a person possesses. Neither do I want them rejecting a friendship because of what a person lacks.

I guarantee you that the peripheral aspects of who we are will change, but the core of who we are remains unbroken. Many things have changed about my physical appearance over the past eighteen years. But I am still the woman my husband met in 1990; the parts of me that really matter are intact.

Many times multiple hurts and disappointments can cause us to build up walls around our hearts. But I believe the nucleus of who we are is still there and can shine through if we let it. Our core, what makes us who we are, remains constant though we are faced with many challenges over our lifetime.

Tragic experiences can change you. Life will harden you if you let it. Look deep inside and pull out the real you. If you do not like the real you, talk to God about it. He has a way of transforming lives.

> *Do not conform any longer to the pattern of this world, but be transformed by the renewing of your mind. Then you will be able to test and approve what God's will is— his good, pleasing and perfect will* (Romans 12:2).

And we, who with unveiled faces all reflect the Lord's glory, are being transformed into his likeness with ever-increasing glory, which comes from the Lord, who is the Spirit **(2 Corinthians 3:18).**

When we look at others, we have to be able to look beyond the fancy clothes and the expensive car. We have to look beyond the plush gated community that people live in and see the real person. Many people behind those gates are lost and unhappy. Their lives are filled with loneliness even though they have all this world can give them. Many of them are beautiful, but they do not realize it because they are looking in the wrong mirror. They are looking in the mirror that says, "If you do not look like someone famous, or if you do not have what others have, then you are not beautiful."

If you want to know your true value, look in the mirror of God's Word. No matter what form of corrective lens you wear, you cannot see my real beauty. The part of me that tells you who I really am cannot be seen with the naked eye. When you look at me, you only see the external. The real beauty of who I am goes deeper than the eyes can see.

Friends, we must know who we are. We must have confidence in the Word of God and believe what God says about us. The external beauty fades with time, but God's Word will never pass away. That is why we see so many beautiful old people. Their physical characteristics are not what we are looking at. We are looking at the soul, the spirit, the essence of who that grandmother or grandfather is.

I Am Beautiful

Heaven and earth will pass away but my words will never pass away (Matthew 24:35).

Charm is deceptive, and beauty is fleeting; but a woman who fears the LORD is to be praised (Proverbs 31:30).

My prayer today is that you begin to use the Word of God as your standard and know without a shadow of a doubt that you are beautiful based on what God says about you.

The story of Esther is one of my favorite books in the Bible.

*Let the king appoint commissioners in every province of his realm to bring all these **beautiful** girls into the harem at the citadel of Susa. Let them be placed under the care of Hegai, the king's eunuch, who is in charge of the women; and let beauty treatments be given to them* (Esther 2:3, emphasis added).

Esther was among the young women chosen to enter the beauty regimen designed to prepare them to become queen. They were placed under the care of the king's eunuch. The grooming process included six months with oil of myrrh and six months with perfumes. Each girl was taken into the king after she had completed twelve months of preparation. While it is true that Esther was very beautiful externally, she was also beautiful inside. She found favor in the sight of everyone she encountered.

After twelve months of beauty treatments, each girl was

permitted to spend one night with the king. If the girl was sent back and never called for again, she was destined to live as though she was a widow for the remainder of her life. (See 2 Samuel 20:3.)

I imagine that with the large number of virgins waiting, it took a while for each of them to get their night with the king. In fact, it is believed to have taken the king three years before he got to Esther. The Scripture states that Esther was taken to King Ahasuerus in the royal palace during the tenth month of his seventh year.

The Scripture records that the king loved Esther above all the women, and she became the wife of the king four years after Queen Vashti and King Ahasuerus were divorced.

Esther was a woman who would use her position to fulfill her destiny. She realized that life was more than looks. She knew her beauty was deeper than what you could see on the outside. Esther did not feel she would be chosen as queen. She did not consider herself as beautiful as the other women in the "program."

The king saw something in her that she did not see in herself. Many times others will see our true beauty when we do not see it. Often it will take others to speak into our lives for us to see it. God will use other people to give you confidence. God will use you to support others; and when you encourage others, you are encouraging yourself.

We need people around us who can encourage us and who will tell us the truth. Everyone needs a little push sometimes. We need people in our lives who will cause us to strive to become everything that God has created us to be.

One of my spiritual callings is to position people for destiny. Quite often we know what we should be doing, but we need someone to give us a little shove. My role is to encourage others to seek God for answers. We should not allow others to speak negative words over our lives.

Your heavenly Father thinks you are beautiful. Did you know that He has been drawing and wooing you to Himself before you came forth from your mother's womb? God loved you from the beginning of time.

> *The LORD appeared to us in the past, saying: "I have loved you with an everlasting love; I have drawn you with loving-kindness"* (Jeremiah 31:3).

Nothing you can do or say will change the way God feels about you. Even when you do ugly things, He still loves you. When you do not love Him back, He keeps on loving you. God sees your real beauty. He sees the real you, not the made up you or the counterfeit you. When your heavenly Father looks at you, He sees His creation.

Real beauty does not come from spending hours in the hair salon. You cannot purchase true beauty at the cosmetic counter. Contrary to what we have been led to believe, ladies, beauty does not come in a box or a jar.

However, we should keep ourselves fit and healthy. God expects us to take good care of our bodies. We all want our bodies to be around and useful for a long time. But in our quest to maintain a healthy exterior, we should not neglect to give equal attention to the interior. Equal attention must be given to the fixing up of the spirit man as well as the natural man.

When we want to lose weight, sometimes we just stop eating without giving attention to the importance of what we eliminate. When we fail to eat the proper nutrition, our strength is diminished. We become unable to process information as quickly as we would if we were eating a balanced and healthy diet.

Learning is also diminished when we do not take in the proper nutrients. When we do not include adequate protein in our diet, we have less energy. We may start out strong, but we will burn out fast. We will begin to feel sluggish early in the day.

That is similar to what happens when we are on a spiritual diet. We lose weight spiritually. We are not as powerful in pulling down strongholds and are not as strong when we have to stand up to the enemy. Let's be equal opportunity people by giving our spiritual bodies as much attention as we give our natural bodies.

When we understand that our true beauty is internal, we will value our heart condition as much as we value the part of us that others see. As we gain new insight and understanding of how God looks at us, we will begin to position ourselves correctly. We will begin to put more emphasis on the internal and less on the external.

I Am Beautiful

Plastic surgery is a booming business now, and probably you or someone you know has had work done. I am by no means opposed to plastic surgery. I have not ruled it out for myself at some point in my life. However, I could caution anyone considering plastic surgery to examine their reasons for doing so. Is it to be accepted by someone? Is it so others will think you are beautiful? What are your real motivations for wanting to alter what has been a natural progression?

If you are trying to fix the outside without doing the necessary inside work, you will still be unhappy. You cannot fix part of yourself without paying attention to the other part. You are beautiful to God. Beauty is in the eyes of the beholder.

Let us pray.

Dear Heavenly Father,

Today, I hold up the mirror of your Word before me. I want to see myself as You see me. Father, I ask that You would take this Word and help me to apply it to my life. Help me to know that I am uniquely designed by You. I close my ears to what society tells me about how I look. I open my heart to what You say in Your Word about me. I use Your Word now to examine my heart; if there is anything in my heart that does not look beautiful to You. I ask that you remove it now. Father, I thank you for loving me, and I declare that I am beautiful. Amen.

CHAPTER FOUR

I Am the Righteousness of God

Not only is your identity important to you, but it is also important to the thief who wants to steal it from you. The thief wants to use your name, credit cards, and social security number. He wants to charge things to your name and leave you with a large stack of bills.

Usually when a person uses another person's identity, it is because he or she is unable to secure what they want by using their own identity. Some people will go to great lengths to steal the name and identity of another person if it will make them more acceptable to other people.

Just a few days ago, my husband received a very large Sprint bill that had been sent to collections. He has never owned a Sprint account. When he checked into it, he found that he had been the victim of identity theft. Someone used my husband's information to obtain something they could not obtain on their own.

Many times we wear clothes we cannot afford and drive cars we cannot pay for just to have the approval of people. Strangely most of the time we either do not know or do not like the people we are trying to impress.

Most of us go through life thinking we know who we are but in reality we do not. If you ask many people who they are, they would identify themselves by their profession or by their trade. Friends, if you allow your jobs or others to define who you are, you will have a mistaken identity.

When you receive Jesus Christ as Lord and Savior, you have a new identity. This new identity in Christ solves the dilemma of acceptance. When you understand who you are in Christ, you realize that you have already been accepted by God, and no one can improve on that! You have been made righteous through Christ Jesus. You are totally forgiven. Christ has accepted you, and that is all that matters.

> *I have been crucified with Christ and I no longer live, but Christ lives in me. The life I live in the body, I live by faith in the Son of God, who loved me and gave himself for me. I do not set aside the grace of God, for if righteousness could be gained through the law, Christ died for nothing!* (Galatians 3:20-21)

Apart from Christ, we cannot be called righteous. We cannot gain righteousness through good deeds. Because of Christ's death on the cross, we have been declared righteous.

I Am the Righteousness of God

Let's look at what happens when one uses another's identity to accomplish or acquire what he cannot obtain on his own. Depending on the status of the victim, the thief may gain access to elite clubs. He may be able to purchase items he could have only dreamed of purchasing before stealing the victim's identity.

That is what Christ did for us on the cross. We could not obtain a righteous status on our own. He died on the cross for our sins and declared us righteous. He gave us His identity. We have been made righteous through the blood of Jesus Christ. The difference is that Christ gave us His identity while the thief steals our identity.

With your identity comes privileges. When the thief identifies himself as you, and if he can prove it, he is entitled to whatever you own. He can use your name, your social security number, and your identification. In other words, he can have access to everything you own.

Many years ago I was the victim of identity theft. The person used my identity to acquire something he could not acquire on his own. Many people now have something called identity thief protection. This protects them against someone stealing their identity. Christ offers us protection as well. If we continue to draw near to Him, the enemy cannot steal who we are.

When we have been declared righteous by our Savior, we have His permission to use His name. We can use His name for healing, for blessing, and for anything we ask according to

His will. We do not have to steal Christ's identity. He gives us His identity when we accept Him as Lord and Savior of our lives. We become the righteousness of God.

> *Therefore confess your sins to each other and pray for each other so that you may be healed. The prayer of a righteous man is powerful and effective* (James 5:16).

We are not righteous in ourselves. We are righteous because of Jesus' death on the cross. He died to take away our sins, and we take on His righteousness.

The word *righteous* means "acting in accordance with divine or moral law; to be free from guilt or sin." The only reason we are free from guilt or sin is because Christ took our sins to the cross. He died for us, even though He had not sinned. He took our punishment and gave us His righteousness.

Even as I write this, my heart is overjoyed to know that I was loved with this unconditional love. God sent His Son, Jesus Christ, who knew no sin to become sin for us.

> *For he hath made him to be **sin** for us, who **knew no sin**; that we might be made the righteousness of God in him* (2 Corinthians 5:21 KJV, emphasis added).

> *Being then made free from **sin**, ye **became** the servants of righteousness* (Romans 6:18 KJV, emphasis added).

Our righteousness is in Him. Our righteousness is because of Him. Without Christ we are nothing. Without

I Am the Righteousness of God

Him we can do nothing. I thank God for giving His only Son to die for the sins of the world.

"This is the covenant I will make with them after that time," says the Lord. "I will put my laws in their hearts, and I will write them on their minds." Then he adds: "Their sins and lawless acts I will remember no more." And where these have been forgiven, there is no longer any sacrifice for sin (Hebrews 10:16).

When talking about righteousness, it is important that we understand that not only have we been declared righteous, but also we must live a righteous lifestyle. We must strive to be in right standing with God. We must practice the principles of His Word. Our ways must be pleasing to God. Once we have been forgiven of our sins, we must seek to do the things that bring glory and honor to His name. Our salvation was purchased at no cost to us, but Jesus paid the price with His life.

Even though Christ died on the cross and forgave our sins, you may ask why we still need to confess our sins. Yes, our sins were forgiven at Calvary. Our past, present, and future sins were all dealt with at the cross. Jesus' death was the sacrifice needed to redeem man back to God.

Receiving Jesus as Lord of our lives does not mean that we will never sin again. The sacrifice that Jesus made on the cross was the finished work. No one has to die every time we sin. What Jesus did on the cross was enough to cover our past, present, and future sins. This does not mean that we have a license to practice willful sin. It does mean that if we sin, we can be forgiven because of the precious blood of Jesus that was shed on Calvary.

Without the shedding of blood there is no forgiveness (Hebrews 9:22).

My little children, these things write I unto you, that ye sin not. And if any man sin, we have an advocate with the Father, Jesus Christ the righteous (1 John 2:1 KJV).

Not only has Christ declared us righteous, but He has called us to be holy. What does it mean to be holy? Many times we think living holy is what the world sees us do. The call to be holy is more about the transformation of our hearts than an external demonstration. Once our hearts have been transformed, I believe the change will be visible in our lifestyle.

For it is written: "Be holy, because I am holy" (1 Peter 1:16).

God is calling believers to holiness. Many Christians do not take seriously the call to be holy. In 1 Peter 1:13-16 we see God is indeed calling us to be holy:

Therefore gird up the loins of your mind, be sober, and rest your hope fully upon the grace that is to be brought to you at the revelation of Jesus Christ; as obedient children, not conforming yourselves to the former lusts, as in your ignorance; but as He who called you is holy, you also be holy in all your conduct, because it is written, "Be holy, for I am holy."

I Am the Righteousness of God

The Scripture records in 2 Timothy 1:8-9,

So do not be ashamed to testify about our Lord, or ashamed of me his prisoner. But join with me in suffering for the gospel, by the power of God, who has saved us and called us to a holy life—not because of anything we have done but because of his own purpose and grace. This grace was given us in Christ Jesus before the beginning of time.

In this Scripture Timothy is encouraged not to be ashamed of what God has done in his life. Most of the apostles faced opposition, and some died as a result of their testimony. Paul is concerned that Timothy might be afraid to witness. He is calling Timothy to be bold. God's call to believers today is for boldness. However, he also wants us to know that our salvation is not based on works. It is impossible to earn our way into heaven. Salvation is according to God's own purpose and plan.

God is holy and everything that refers to Him is holy. Holiness is the very essence of who He is. Our lives should always exemplify what Jesus' life was like when He lived on earth.

Holiness is the quality of life. It should not be confused with righteousness, which means right standing with God. When you were born again, you were made the righteousness of God through Jesus Christ. Because we have been made righteous through Jesus Christ, we choose to live holy. We choose a holy lifestyle every day. At times this may be a difficult choice, but it is one we have to make each day. Every morning we need to make a conscience decision to live holy, irregardless of what is going on around us. It does not matter what I have to face; I need to deal with it as a holy man or woman of God.

While it is true we are not Jesus and we are sinful beings, we can strive to be like Him. Our goal as believers should be to strive to be more like Jesus every day. Yes, I messed up yesterday, but I am going to try again today. I realize I cannot do it on my own. I need more of God to be more like Him.

Many of the people of the Bible suffered as we do today. They had to face challenging times in their lives. When Paul asked the Lord about what was going on in his life, the Scripture records the following:

But he said to me, "My grace is sufficient for you, for my power is made perfect in weakness." Therefore I will boast all the more gladly about my weaknesses, so that Christ's power may rest on me (2 Corinthians 12:9**).**

His grace is always available to help us. When we are without strength, we look to the Lord. He will provide power by His grace. That is why we must genuinely seek Him moment by moment.

When we are weak, He gives us the strength we need to make it a little farther. Many days we will miss the mark, but what matters is that we are moving in the right direction. My father used to say, "Aim for the stars. You may never reach them, but as long as you aim for the stars, you will not hit anything on the ground." In our striving, we may never reach the height we desire, but we will reach a point higher than where we started.

I Am the Righteousness of God

When we look at our lives in relationship to the life of Christ, we know His life was holy because Satan tried to tempt Him. We will know when we are pleasing God, because Satan will try to tempt us as well. Strive to live a holy life. Strive to be more like Jesus every day. The tempter will come after you, but we can use God's Word to fight him.

Jesus was tempted by Satan. The temptation of Jesus is not an effort on the part of the devil to entice Jesus into committing sin. It was more of an effort to compel Jesus to set aside His complete obedience to the will and purpose of God by adopting an easier means to the fulfillment of His mission.

Satan did not lead Jesus into the temptation. He was led there by the Holy Spirit. The Scripture does not say that Satan appeared in the flesh to Jesus. Satan would have appeared in Jesus' mind just as he appears to us today.

The most profound attack of the enemy in the life of a believer is the attack of the mind. That is why it is so important to keep our mind on Jesus. We need to feed our minds with the Word of God daily. The enemy seeks to discourage the people of God. If he can make us feel like we are not who God says we are, he has succeeded.

Satan's temptation of Jesus while He was in the wilderness is recorded in Matthew chapter four. This temptation took place immediately after Jesus' baptism.

At that time Jesus came from Nazareth in Galilee and was baptized by John in the Jordan. As Jesus was coming up out of the water, he saw heaven being torn open and the Spirit descending on him like a dove. And a voice came from heaven: "You are my Son, whom I love; with you I am well pleased." At once the Spirit sent him out into the desert (Mark 1:9-12).

Spiritual victories are often followed by the testing of our faith. Many of our greatest battles are faced just as we are in a position to do something great for God. As you read Matthew's account of the temptation of Jesus in the fourth chapter, we see many things happening.

Jesus' response to all three temptations was from the Word of God. Jesus wanted to show us as believers the power of God's Word to combat the enemy. Jesus' experience serves as an example to us when we face spiritual warfare today.

When you are ready to walk in the will of God for your life, Satan will come after you. Just think back over some of the most prevalent attacks of the enemy on you. Was it while you were idling wasting time or was it when you were about to do something big for God? In my life, anytime I am about to step out in faith to go to the next level, the attacks from the enemy escalate.

The devil knows when God is up to something in your life. He turns up the heat to try to get you to give up before you even begin. Remember the enemy does not like the fact that you are the righteousness of God. He would rather see you with your head hung down in shame than to live in victory.

Jesus Christ was our example. We can overcome the

enemy by recognizing false teaching. When the enemy tells us something that we know is not true according to the Word of God, we must refuse to follow it.

You, dear children, are from God and have overcome them, because the one who is in you is greater than the one who is in the world (1 John 4:4).

Even as I write this book, I recognize that I am under an attack. Why? Because I am doing something that I believe God has commissioned me to do. Whenever you make up your mind to fulfill God's call on your life, the enemy will try to stop you.

I have memories of hearing testimonies from people in church saying, "The devil is trying to stop me." I did not really understand what they meant. I was a Christian, and things seemed to be going well for me. I wondered why I was not being bothered by the enemy.

The moment I stepped up and said publicly, "I am going to do whatever God wants me to do," the enemy heard it. Oh my friend, Satan only wants to stop you if you are doing something that will make a difference in the kingdom. If Satan is not trying to stop you, then you must not be doing anything.

No matter what Satan tempted Jesus with, or how often he tempted Him, Jesus never yielded to him. The Scripture tells us to resist as well.

Submit yourselves, then, to God. Resist the devil, and he will flee from you (James 4:7).

When we resist the temptation that the evil one throws our way, he will have no choice but to flee. We belong to God, and as long as we maintain our proper identity, the enemy must leave us just as he left Jesus in the wilderness.

What Jesus did for us sanctified us once and for all through His blood. When we have received Him as Savior, sin will no longer control our lives. Sin must not be a habit of our lives.

If we deliberately keep on sinning after we have received the knowledge of the truth, no sacrifice for sins is left, but only a fearful expectation of judgment and of raging fire that will consume the enemies of God (Hebrews 10:26).

The reference in this Scripture about sin is not about an occasional act of sin. Here the Word of God is talking about willful sin. A person who consciously rejects God is willfully sinning. To sin intentionally after receiving the understanding of the truth is apostasy.

There will be times, however, when we will choose to go our own way instead of the way of righteousness. There will be times when we fail in our lives. We will experience broken relationships in our lives. Sometimes we will say things we should not say and act in a way that is not according to God's Word.

It is important that we repent when we realize we are not obeying God's Word. Repentance is a complete turn around, not just in words, but with the heart. Our hearts need to be

I Am the Righteousness of God

changed. Many times we may say that we repented, but we continue to walk in the same direction.

True repentance brings a change in our hearts. Our desires change; we turn from the sin and focus on the Savior. Repentance is to display godly sorrow for our sins and not plan to repeat that sin again. We ask that He forgive us and help us to follow His Word.

I have been declared righteous because Christ died for me, and I have asked Him to forgive me and cleanse me of all unrighteousness. We cannot save ourselves. Although God shows us in His Word how we should live, none of us can live righteously without God being at the center of our lives. The Scripture teaches that we all have sinned. It is only through our hope and faith in Jesus Christ that we are made righteous.

For all have sinned and fall short of the glory of God (Romans 3:23).

We must understand that our righteousness is not because of anything we have done, but it is because of what Christ has done.

Therefore no one will be declared righteous in his sight by observing the law; rather, through the law we become conscious of sin (Romans 3:20).

The only way to be righteous is through faith.

God made him who had no sin to be sin for us, so that in

him we might become the righteousness of God (2 Corinthians 5:21).

In faith we claim the goodness of Jesus, and then God puts this to our account. Jesus' obedience is accepted in place of our mistakes God accepts and pardons us because of what Jesus has done. When Jesus died on the cross for our sins, we were pardoned. Now all we have to do is accept His pardon by confessing our sins and receiving His forgiveness.

We were dead in our trespasses and sins until Jesus Christ made us alive by His death on the cross.

Buried with Him in baptism, in which you also were raised with Him through faith in the working of God who raised Him from the dead. And you being dead in your trespasses and the uncircumcision of your flesh, He has made alive together with Him having forgiven you all trespasses (Colossians 2:12-13 NKJV).

Buried in baptism is the symbol of the believer's association with Christ's death on the cross. Water baptism itself does not bring forgiveness of sins. Baptism is considered to be the outward sign of salvation. When Jesus forgives our sins, Scripture tells us that our sins have been cast into the "depths of the sea."

You will again have compassion on us; you will tread our sins underfoot and hurl all our iniquities into the depths of the sea (Micah 7:19).

Corrie ten Boom said, "He puts up a sign, saying, No

I Am the Righteousness of God

fishing allowed." Corrie ten Boom knew something about forgiveness since she was a Holocaust survivor of the Hitler regime. Her family did not survive. They were Dutch Christians arrested by the Nazis for hiding Jews in their home. She watched the horrors of the genocide in Ravensbruck concentration camp and barely survived.

Following the war, she became famous for her book, *The Hiding Place*, in which she shared the story of her family. She traveled the world, speaking and sharing her faith with thousands of people. I was so moved when I read about Corrie and her awesome story of forgiveness.

One night she spoke about the reality of Christ forgiving us. Afterwards a man came forward to speak to her. She recognized him as a guard from Ravensbruck. She instantly felt all the hatred and pain from the terror of those years of persecution. He told her he had been moved by her talk on forgiveness, and crying, he asked if he might receive the forgiveness of Christ of which she had spoken. In herself she could not offer that forgiveness. She remembered the command of Christ to love your enemy and to forgive seventy times seven the person who has wronged you. When Peter asked how many times would he have to forgive his brother who had sinned against him,

*Jesus answered, "I tell you, not **seven times**, but up to **seventy times seven**"* (Matthew 18:22 NKJ, emphasis added).

As Corrie prayed that Jesus would give her the strength

to forgive the man, she felt a sensation begin in her heart and flow through her hand as it touched his. Then she heard herself saying, "In the name of Jesus Christ, I forgive you."

The man fell at her feet and wept a prayer of thanks. The power of God's forgiveness is amazing to me. Every time I read her story, I ask myself if I could do the same thing. I realize on my own I would never be able to offer that kind of forgiveness. With the power of God working in my life, however, all things are possible.

As far as the east is from the west, so has he removed our transgressions from us (Psalm 103:12).

It does not matter how bad you think you have been, God will forgive you. Not only will He forgive you, but He chooses not to remember your sins. If God does not remember them, I refuse to let anyone else hold my sins over my head.

I was just thinking the other day of an incident that happened to me. I felt that I had been emotionally abused by another person. Each time I would think of the event that had occurred, the painful feeling would resurface. I began to pray and ask God to help me to forgive the person who had offended me. My flesh said, "You were right, and they were wrong." But I knew if I was to be a vessel that God would honor, I had to forgive.

Being able to release God's promises in our lives is so important. The way we release blessings in our lives is to not allow sin to take root in our hearts. If we allow sin to take

I Am the Righteousness of God

root, it will form bitterness. When bitterness has developed, it will lock the door to our blessings. Our hearts will become cold and hard toward people and their needs.

I remind my children often of their rich spiritual inheritance. They are the seed of the righteous. They come from a long line of men and women of God. My husband and I have a long list of forefathers who helped blaze the trail to organized religion as we know it today.

I thank God for those who stood in the gap for me many generations before I came on the scene. My deepest desire is to leave the same legacy for those who will come after me—not only my children whom I have birthed naturally, but also to everyone in whose lives God has allowed me the privilege to sow seeds.

When we walk in obedience to do what God has asked us to do, we leave a righteous legacy for our children. You and I have been made righteous by the precious blood of Jesus Christ. Now that we have been made righteous, it is our responsibility to bring others to Christ. When Jesus blots out our transgressions, He said He would not remember them. If He has done that for us, we must try to do the same for others who have hurt us.

I, even I, am he who blots out your transgressions, for my own sake, and remembers your sins no more (Isaiah 43:25).

I have been made righteous in Christ Jesus. Therefore, I am the righteousness of God.

Let us pray.

Dear Heavenly Father,

I thank You for the awesome sacrifice of giving Your Son, Jesus, to die on the cross for my sins. Because of Your love for me, I have been made righteous. I thank You for the privilege You have given me to be born anew. I ask now that You would teach me how to share that same love with everyone that I meet. Thank You for Your forgiveness of my sins, and please let me show the same forgiveness to others. In Jesus' name I pray. Amen.

CHAPTER FIVE

I Am Prosperous

When I was a much younger woman, I heard the prosperity message. The preacher would say, "God wants to bless you. He wants you to live the abundant life." I would look at those who deemed themselves prosperous as Christians and think that I must not be doing something right.

I did not have the fancy clothes, the fat bank account, nor the luxury car that some people did. This misunderstood message set me on a road to look prosperous. Notice, I did not say it put me on a road to be prosperous because I just wanted to look like the people around me who fit the prosperous definition.

I would shop every week, buying new clothes using credit cards. I purchased my dream sports car. Accumulating stuff, I was thinking it would answer the longings of my heart. I really believe that is one of the reasons so many of us are in such huge debt. We want instant gratification; no one wants to wait for anything anymore.

The church is as much to blame as the world because we teach that prosperity gospel. We make people feel that if they do not have what other have, they must be doing something wrong. Friends, let me assure you that God's focus is not on your material possessions.

I want to share with you the truth of God's Word as it relates to prosperity. It has less to do with your wallet and more to do with your soul. What does God's Word say about my prosperity? In Scripture we find many references.

God's desire for us is that we be whole in every area of our lives. It is not His will that we are lacking in any part of our lives. We must trust God and rely on Him. Many times we put our trust in man and are disappointed. God never fails. We can always count on Him to perform His Word.

Beloved, I wish above all things that thou mayest prosper and be in health, even as thy soul prospereth (3 John 1:2 KJV).

The Scripture teaches that God's desire for us is that we thrive. When we talk about prospering from God's perspective, it is not about money. When we look at the meaning of the above Scripture, it has nothing to do with financial prosperity. John's greeting in this verse simply follows the pattern of greetings common to a Greek letter. The author, John, is not saying that wealth and riches should be considered as the supreme gifts of life. He is just saying that his wish is that all is well with Gaius, the recipient of his letter. It is merely a desire expressed and not a promise that is given by the apostle to a fellow believer.

Many prosperity teachers would have you believe that it is all about how much money you have. I disagree because prosperity is a wholeness word. Prosperity means nothing is missing, nothing is broken, and nothing is lacking.

The apostle John is saying that in the same way that your soul walks in a proper and right manner, his wish is that everything about Gaius is doing well and that he is healthy. John is saying that doing well and being healthy depends upon the right direction of one's soul and one's attitude.

Our heavenly Father wants the best for us. The question is, what is best for us? What may be best for one may not be good for another. Our concentration should be less about material things and more about spiritual things. I heard someone say, "We are spiritual beings having a human experience." We tend to focus on being human beings most of the time and on having a spiritual experience only every now and then.

Our main focus needs to be, "Who did God create me to be?" When we walk in and live in the spirit, our interest in material things will be less. Living in the spirit is not about how many material things we have; it is about our needs being met and having the ability to meet the needs of others.

On the first day of every week, each one of you should set aside a sum of money in keeping with his income, saving it up, so that when I come no collections will have to be made (1 Corinthians 16:2).

The above Scripture is used in regards to the giving of benevolence to the church. Although it is translated as "God hath prospered him," we should not get the idea that this prospering necessarily means riches. It means as the Lord has made provision for the believer, in the same measure the believer should also lay aside a matching offering. The idea of wealth is really missing from the word "prosper."

The LORD will grant you abundant prosperity—in the fruit of your womb, the young of your livestock and the crops of your ground—in the land he swore to your forefathers to give you (Deuteronomy 28:11**)**.

God will prosper you in every area of your life. When you walk in obedience to God's Word, you will not suffer lack. When I refer to suffering lack, I do not mean never bouncing a check or never being late on a bill. I am talking about your needs being supplied.

Many times we confuse our needs with our desires. You might say paying my electric bill is a big need. Yes, I agree it is a need, but what did you buy that you did not need that caused you not to have enough for your electric bill? We must understand the choices we make in our lives.

See I set before you today life and prosperity, death and destruction (Deuteronomy 30:15**)**.

God gives us free will, and we sometimes make choices that cause us to live beneath our privilege. If we act in obedience, we can receive everything God's Word has promised us.

The Scripture teaches us in Job 36:11,

*If they obey and serve him, they will spend the rest of their days in **prosperity** and their years in contentment* (emphasis added).

What an awesome promise from God! In exchange for obeying and serving Him, we will spend our days in prosperity and years in contentment. Now, remember we already established that prosperity is not money alone. The word prosperity is referred to in Scripture many times, but what does it really mean?

Many of the prosperity Scriptures we read teach us how God deals with His people. If we are obedient to what God says, we will have wisdom, peace, calmness, and rewards. Remember, prosperity is a wholeness word. The prosperity in the Scriptures is not focused on money. The wisdom that God will give us is our prosperity. I believe for most of us, we do not have a money problem anyway. We lack wisdom, and as a result, our finances are in disarray.

Instead of praying for financial blessings, we need to pray for wisdom. If we have the wisdom of God, we can handle our finances. When we have the peace of God, we will not overreact when our cash is low. We will remain calm and learn to trust God.

Being prosperous is not what my portfolio says about me or what man thinks about me. I constantly remind myself that I am who God says I am. To be prosperous means to be successful. What is your definition of success? I believe one definition of success is to have the prosperity of God.

Sometimes we hear extreme teaching on this subject. There have been those that have made the mistake of trying to exaggerate what God is actually doing. I believe God wants us to live wholesome and moderate lives that glorify Him, without taking attention away from what He is doing. Many Christians are so confused, but the truth is we do not need to be overly concerned about being prosperous.

Put to death, therefore, whatever belongs to your earthly nature: sexual immorality, impurity, lust, evil desires and greed, which is idolatry (Colossians 3:5).

The meaning of the Greek word for greed is an "eager and constant desire for more ... a craving desire for more than we need." Greed is idolatry. It is a fixation for something else that will come between us and the Lord.

Those who cling to worthless idols forfeit the grace that could be theirs (Jonah 2:8).

When we are not in a right relationship with God, even as Christians, we are destroying ourselves. The Scripture teaches that God will supply our needs. We need to focus more on the supplier and less on the supplies.

The Word of God always challenges us as Christians to

be giving and loving to others. When we are greedy, it is hard to be generous. That is why it is so important for us to understand the word *prosperity* as it relates to God and spiritual things. It is more of a blessing to give than to receive.

> *In everything I did, I showed you that by this kind of hard work we must help the weak, remembering the words the Lord Jesus himself said: "It is more blessed to give than to receive"* (Acts 20:35).

We must look at things through our spiritual eyes. We can question the truth of God's Word, but it does not change God's Word.

> *Upon the first day of the week let every one of you lay by him in store, as God hath prospered him, that there be no gatherings when I come* (1 Corinthians 16:2 KJV).

Here Paul is again addressing a question from the Corinthians about giving. The first day of the week was the regular meeting day of the early church, which is similar to what we do today. When Paul talks about putting aside as God hath prospered, he is speaking of Christian giving. This would be what we consider tithes and offerings in most churches today.

Paul is simply saying, as God hath prospered you, give your offering. The offerings were to be collected before Paul arrived so that he would not need to pressure the people when he saw them.

> *Making request, if by any means now at length I might*

have a prosperous journey by the will of God to come unto you (Romans 1:10 KJV).

Notice the word *prosper* here. It is from the Greek word *euodoo,* which means, "to help on one's way, a way or journey; to have a prosperous journey."

God wants to bless us and meet our needs, but when we are greedy, we distort the intent of God's prosperity for our lives. It is not God's plan that we live in greed but in godly contentment. God does not want us to complain about what we do not have. He does not want us to stress ourselves out trying to keep up with the Joneses. We have to be content with what we have. We must reach a godly balance in our lives. "Give us this day our daily bread"—tomorrow is not promised to us. We only have today; let tomorrow take care of itself.

In fact, when we read about the apostle Paul in Romans 1:10, his prosperous journey to Rome was not what most of us would call prosperous. He was shipwrecked and bitten by a snake along his prosperous journey. But was his journey prosperous in the eyes of God? What were his motives? Did he accomplish his goals in the process?

Your prosperity is determined many times by your motive. If you have selfish motives, you may have millions of dollars and not be prosperous. If you have your needs met, give millions away to others, and your motives are right, then you are prosperous.

How do I learn to be content when others around me

have so much and I have so little? Discontent is the natural fiber of who we are. Every day we find more things to make us feel dissatisfied. We pass a nicer car on the road. We see a bigger house in our neighborhood. Someone gets the promotion we wanted.

> *I know what it is to be in need, and I know what it is to have plenty. I have learned the secret of being content in any and every situation, whether well fed or hungry, whether living in plenty or in want* (Philippians 4:11-12).

When we know God loves us and that He will provide for us, we can be satisfied with what we have. We can also be content with who we are. Contentment is a learned behavior, something that we need to practice. We can behave our way to success. (I will cover more in the upcoming chapters regarding contentment.)

I want to show you how you can be prosperous in every area of your life. Prosperity is a wholeness word, including spiritual, physical, material, emotional, and social.

Spiritual Prosperity

My deepest desire for prosperity is spiritual. The Lord wants us to experience spiritual prosperity. Our soul prospers when we are in a right relationship with our Lord and Savior Jesus Christ. It would profit us nothing to gain prosperity in other areas of our lives and lack prosperity in our spirit. The Scripture teaches that man does not live by bread alone.

> *Jesus answered, "It is written: 'Man does not live on bread alone, but on every word that comes from the mouth of God'"* (Luke 4:4).

> *Love the Lord your God with all your heart and with all your soul and with all your strength* (Deuteronomy 6:5).

> *Jesus replied: "Love the Lord your God with all your heart and with all your soul and with all your mind." This is the first and greatest commandment. And the second is like it: "Love your neighbor as yourself All the Law and the Prophets hang on these two commandments"* (Matthew 22:37-40).

Our souls will begin to prosper when we receive a spirit of wisdom and revelation to know the Lord better. Our hearts must be open to know God's plan and purpose for our lives. We must understand the rich inheritance that we have as children of God.

> *Now if we are children, then we are heirs—heirs of God and co-heirs with Christ, if indeed we share in his sufferings in order that we may also share in his glory* (Romans 8:17).

We must receive the enormous power of God that is available to us.

> *Now to him who is able to do immeasurably more than all we ask or imagine, according to his power that is at work within us* (Ephesians 3:20).

His love for us is so incredible that we cannot begin to grasp the concept of just how much He loves us. Our desire must be to have more of God. Our quest to know Him better will motivate us to seek after Him. As we study the Word of God, we will grow spiritually. This is the prosperity we seek first and foremost.

No, in all these things we are more than conquerors through him who loved us. For I am convinced that neither death nor life, neither angels nor demons, neither the present nor the future, nor any powers, neither height nor depth, nor anything else in all creation, will be able to separate us from the love of God that is in Christ Jesus our Lord (Romans 8:37-39).

Understanding this kind of love is the spiritual prosperity that the Lord wants us to experience. Even though we cannot really understand this kind of love, it is available to all who ask today.

Physical Prosperity

God wants us to experience physical prosperity. He wants to heal us of all diseases and to redeem our lives from destruction. In Scripture we read of how Jesus took our infirmities and carried our diseases.

Who forgives all your sins and heals all your diseases, who redeems your life from the pit and crowns you with love and compassion, who satisfies your desires with good things so that your youth is renewed like the eagle's (Psalm 103:3-5).

God's desire is that we be totally healed of sickness and diseases.

Jesus went throughout Galilee, teaching in their synagogues, preaching the good news of the kingdom, and healing every disease and sickness among the people (Matthew 4:23-24).

The Lord has made a covenant of healing with us when we obey his commandments.

Worship the LORD your God, and his blessing will be on your food and water. I will take away sickness from among you (Exodus 23:25-26).

He said, "If you listen carefully to the voice of the LORD your God and do what is right in his eyes, if you pay attention to his commands and keep all his decrees, I will not bring on you any of the diseases I brought on the Egyptians, for I am the LORD, who heals you" (Exodus 15:26).

Do not bow down before their gods or worship them or follow their practices. You must demolish them and break their sacred stones to pieces. Worship the LORD your God, and his blessing will be on your food and water. I will take away sickness from among you, and none will miscarry or be barren in your land. I will give you a full life span (Exodus 23:24-26).

When we dedicate our lives to fulfilling God's will and purpose, we can come to the Lord and ask Him to grant us good health. Remember, your healing was prophesied in the Old Testament through the prophet Isaiah:

He was despised and rejected by men, a man of sorrows, and familiar with suffering. Like one from whom men hide their faces he was despised, and we esteemed him not. Surely he took up our infirmities and carried our sorrows, yet we considered him stricken by God, smitten by him, and afflicted. But he was pierced for our transgressions, he was crushed for our iniquities; the punishment that brought us peace was upon him, and by his wounds we are healed (Isaiah 53:3-5).

Material Prosperity

Material things is the area most of our focus is on when it comes to prosperity. Yes it is true that God has promised to meet all our needs.

And my God will meet all your needs according to his glorious riches in Christ Jesus (Philippians 4:19).

God wants us to experience material prosperity, but we must seek Him first.

But seek first his kingdom and his righteousness, and all these things will be given to you as well (Matthew 6:33).

God has promised us a hundredfold blessing for all the sacrifices that we make for His sake.

Peter said to him, "We have left everything to follow you!"

"I tell you the truth," Jesus replied, "no one who has left home or brothers or sisters or mother or father or children or fields for me and the gospel will fail to receive a hundred times as much in this present age (homes, brothers, sisters, mothers, children and fields—and with them, persecutions) and in the age to come, eternal life" (Mark 10:28-30).

Emotional Prosperity

Our heavenly Father wants us to be filled with the joy of the Lord. He will heal our broken hearts and bind up our wounds.

He heals the brokenhearted and binds up their wounds (Psalm 147:3).

He will turn our mourning into dancing and clothe us with joy. He wants to give us beauty for our ashes, the oil of gladness instead of mourning; He wants to give us a garment of praise instead of a spirit of heaviness.

The Spirit of the Sovereign LORD is on me, because the LORD has anointed me to preach good news to the poor. He has sent me to bind up the brokenhearted, to proclaim freedom for the captives and release from darkness for the prisoners, to proclaim the year of the LORD's favor and the day of vengeance of our God, to comfort all who mourn, and provide for those who grieve in Zion to bestow on them a crown of beauty instead of ashes, the oil of gladness instead of mourning, and a garment of praise instead of a spirit of despair. They will be called oaks of righteousness, a planting of the LORD for the display of his splendor (Isaiah 61:1-3).

God wants us to be at peace; He wants us to rest in Him. He has given us His peace. He does not want us to live in fear but to possess His power. God's desire is that our hearts be filled with the fruit of the Spirit. The Lord does not want us to live in sorrow, fear, or pain. He wants to heal our emotions and grant us a life of joy and peace.

There is no fear in love. But perfect love drives out fear, because fear has to do with punishment. The one who fears is not made perfect in love (1 John 4:18).

You will keep in perfect peace him whose mind is steadfast, because he trusts in you (Isaiah 26:3).

Social Prosperity

God wants us to experience social prosperity. He wants us to have meaningful relationships. We draw strength from each other. Relationships are very important to God. The Scripture teaches that we must do everything possible to live at peace with one another.

If it is possible, as far as it depends on you, live at peace with everyone (Romans 12:18).

It is not the will of God that we live lonely, depressed lives. He wants us to be a blessing to those around us and for others to be a blessing to us as well. Jesus called disciples and apostles to assist Him in fulfilling His purpose. No man is an island, and no one stands alone. We need each other. As believers we should be out front, setting the pace for others to follow us as we follow Christ.

> *The LORD will make you the head, not the tail. If you pay attention to the commands of the LORD your God that I give you this day and carefully follow them, you will always be at the top, never at the bottom* (Deuteronomy 28:13).

Friends, God wants you to prosper. His Word tells me that if I follow His commandments I will prosper. Because I am who God says I am, I can stand on His Word and declare that I am prosperous!

I Am Prosperous

Let us pray.

Dear Heavenly Father,

I thank You that You have prospered me. Please forgive me for focusing more on material things than on my relationship with You. I now understand that You are concerned about my whole being. You have made me the head and not the tail. I receive the gift of love that You give to me, and I am thankful in my heart. I declare that I am prosperous in every area of my life. In Jesus' name. Amen.

CHAPTER SIX

I Am Blessed

Matthew 5: The Beatitudes

Now when he saw the crowds, he went up on a mountainside and sat down. His disciples came to him, and he began to teach them saying:

Blessed are the poor in spirit,
  for theirs is the kingdom of heaven.
Blessed are those who mourn,
  for they will be comforted.
Blessed are the meek,
  for they will inherit the earth.
Blessed are those who hunger and thirst for righteousness,
  for they will be filled.
Blessed are the merciful,
  for they will be shown mercy.

I Am Blessed

Blessed are the pure in heart,
for they will see God.
Blessed are the peacemakers,
for they will be called sons of God.
Blessed are those who are persecuted because of righteousness,
for theirs is the kingdom of heaven.
Blessed are you when people insult you, persecute you and
falsely say all kinds of evil against you because of me.
Rejoice and be glad, because great is your reward in
heaven, for in the same way they persecuted the
prophets who were before you.

When we read the Beatitudes, we see a declaration of blessings, an excellence of life, and a reason why the receiver should be considered blessed. The very idea that God blesses us is found throughout Scripture.

What does it mean to be blessed? One definition of blessed is to be happy or contented. Another definition, which I prefer, is to be divinely or supremely favored. I am blessed and highly favored. Yes, according to God's Word, you can be blessed also.

So what is contentment? It is learning to accept what we cannot change. It is having the wisdom to know the difference and the patience to wait when necessary. Content people live longer with less stress and look fresher when you see them. Content people have a fulfilling life, and others enjoy being around them.

If we want to practice contentment, we need to learn to be thankful for what we have. I have a journal that I have kept for the past twenty-five years. I call it my grateful journal. A grateful journal is a place in which you write all the things for which you are thankful.

When I start to feel down about things that are going on in my life, I take out my journal and begin to write some of the things for which I am thankful. Every time I do this, I do not get very far on my list before my mood begins to change. When you think of all the things you have to be thankful for, it is very difficult to be sad.

Learn not to compare yourself to other people. Focus on who you are and what you have to offer the world. You have something special, and no one else can fulfill your assignment. Whatever words God has spoken in your spirit must be obeyed. Many times we depend on others to accomplish our tasks for us.

We look to others to decide if we will be blessed or not. God is more powerful than any man. He will bless whom He pleases. No one else can do what God has commissioned us to do; we need to abide within our calling.

Let every man abide in the same calling wherein he was called **(**1 Corinthians 7:20**).**

So how can I get blessed? Blessings are the result of obedience. When we obey the Word of God, we will be blessed. As long as we abide under divine authority and God's delegated authority, we will be blessed. We have to submit to the authority that God has placed over us. When we submit to authority, we are submitting to God.

Our obedience brings blessing into our lives. When we step out from under authority, we are positioning ourselves for an attack from the enemy. The covering is given to us as protection not as bondage. Many times we see covering as a hindrance to us. We feel restricted in our movement when we have covering on us. But when we need protection from the elements, the covering is nice to have on a cool night.

Man was first blessed by God when he was placed in the garden.

God blessed them and said, "Be fruitful and increase in number and fill the water in the seas, and let the birds increase on the earth" (Genesis 1:22).

Throughout Scripture we read about God blessing people. God wants to bless His people because He loves us so much.

You will be blessed when you come in and blessed when you go out (Deuteronomy 28:6).

God wants to bless us all the time, all day long. The blessings of God are not because we deserve them. We do not work to earn God's blessings. His blessings are given to us because He loves us. The only thing we have to do is obey His Word.

Obedience is the only way we earn blessings. It is not our works; it is the obedience of our hearts. Obeying the Word of God is not always easy. God will ask us to do things that are not pleasing to our flesh. We need to make difficult decisions sometimes if we want to be blessed.

We are often distracted by small disappointments and forget the innumerable blessings we receive from the Lord. Often we are so caught up in what is going wrong in our lives that we forget about the blessings we experience. For example, we become so upset when our car will not start that we forget all the mornings it started without incident. We chastise our children when they disobey us, but we fail to compliment them when they obey.

If we are not careful, negativity can overtake our lives. We become consumed with things that are not going the right way. We lose focus on what is really important in life. When I was growing up, we use to sing a song in church called "Count Your Blessing." The words went something like this:

Count your blessing name them one by one.
Count your blessing see what God has done.
Count your blessing name them one by one
Count your many blessing see what God has done.

Many times we fail to give thanks to God for His many blessings. If the truth be told, there is no way we can name our blessings for there are too many of them. We have an awesome Father who cares so deeply for us. In fact, His love for us runs so deep that He died on the cross for us.

Agape is a Greek word which literally means "love." This is the most commonly used Greek word translated "love" in the New Testament. This love is God's love for us. This is the kind of love that caused God to give His Son to died for us.

(We will more fully address the different kinds of love in Chapter 9, "I Am Loved.")

Many times in my life I have felt down. It seemed as if nothing was going right, or at least not going the way I wanted it to go. But when I wrote in my journal what I was thankful for or read some of the past entries, I felt so much better. I was reminded of how good God is and how much He loves me, and realized that I was blessed. It did not matter what I was dealing with at the time, I was still blessed.

What does it mean to be blessed? Who would you considered a blessed person? Let us see what the Word of God has to say.

> *Blessed is the man who does not walk in the counsel of the wicked or stand in the way of sinners or sit in the seat of mockers. But his delight is in the law of the Lord, and on His law He meditates day and night. He is like a tree planted by streams of water, which yields its fruit in season and whose leaf does not wither. Whatever he does prospers. No so the wicked! They are like chaff that the wind blows away. Therefore, the wicked will not stand in the judgment, nor sinners in the assembly of the righteous. For the Lord watches over the way of the righteous, but the way of the wicked will perish* (Psalm 1:1-6).

We all want to be blessed; I know I do. In Psalms 1 we gain an understanding of what the blessed life is. To be blessed comes through our Lord and Savior Jesus Christ. The Scripture teaches that God will bless those who do not walk in the counsel of the world. When you genuinely pursue a relationship with God, you will be blessed. When you strive to live under God's directions, you will be blessed. If you want to be blessed, make God the center of your life.

This psalm speaks of a righteous person—one who is in the world but not affected by the world. God has a system that is different from the world's system. The world teaches us to get more things to make us happy. The world programs us to try with our own power to make things happen. We live in a democratic society. Many times we mistakenly use our liberties as a way to depend on God less. God is not democratic; He is a more of a dictator. The world does revolve around Him—not the other way around.

The world will tell us that when we have everything we want, we are blessed. God's system is much different than the world's way of thinking. The world's way of thinking takes the focus away from God. Reading the Word of God will helps us to better understand His system.

But seek first his kingdom and his righteousness, and all these things will be given to you as well (Matthew 6:33).

Do you see where the focus is in this Scripture? God's Word says to focus on Him first. We serve a jealous God. He wants His creation to honor Him. We were created to bring glory to God.

When we learn how to enjoy God, we can enjoy His blessing. For those who have never acknowledged Christ in their lives, their feelings of happiness come and go. Feelings change like the wind; they are unstable and unreliable since they have no base or anchor. Only the joy that is found in God can give us true blessings.

In our society today, we often are made to feel that we must not be reliant upon anyone for anything; we must do it all ourselves. We live in an era when the more independent we are, the better off we are. I sometimes believe that when we try so hard to be independent, we are demonstrating our true dependency. We want others to believe that we do not need anyone, but really we are seeking approval from someone.

We have become more financially independent, yet we seek approval. We put stress on ourselves by trying to keep up with other people. We do not want to appear that we are less than anyone else.

Our society has positioned us against God's Word. We choose to believe the lies of the enemy rather than to trust our Creator. God wants to bless us, but we have to abide by His system. When we follow God's system, we are blessed.

If God says we are so blessed, then why are there so many depressed people, Christians included? Every day, we read about or hear about how so many people suffer from depression. Even our children are being medicated for depression. Some are medicated so they will settle down in school. Some children take medication to go to sleep at night or to help them wake up in the morning.

Our world is on an adventure to get people happy. I am

so amazed at our medical community. All you have to do is tell your doctor you have been feeling a little sad, and he will pull out the prescription pad. In our effort to be happy by the world's standards, we are missing a key element. Of course, I know there are chemical disorders of the brain that do require treatment, but let us not be in search of empty happiness. Jesus is the answer to the joy we seek.

By failing to trust in Jesus Christ and to walk in the truth of His Word, we cannot be joyful. We can have everything we could wish for, but if we do not have a relationship with Jesus Christ, we will not feel as though we are blessed. There is an empty place in our souls that can only be satisfied with a relationship with Jesus Christ. Medication will not bring about the joy we seek. Therapy will be fruitless. God is calling us back to Himself. He wants to fill the longing of our hearts. Every empty place, He desires to fill.

O Lord Almighty, blessed is the man who trusts in You (Psalm 84:12).

God will bless us if we trust in Him for our fulfillment. We must not put our trust in the world or in ourselves. When we trust God, we can truly say, "I am blessed."

Jesus admonishes us in Scripture that we cannot do anything without Him.

I am the vine; you are the branches. If a man remains in me and I in him, he will bear much fruit; apart from me, you can do nothing (John 15:5).

We have to be connected to the source if we want to be blessed. Scripture teaches that we are to remain in Him. To remain in Him means to abide in Him. How do I abide in Christ? To abide means to dwell, to stay, and to settle in. The way to abide in Christ is to obey the Word of God. If we obey the Word of God, we will produce fruit.

I learned many years ago that whatever I try to do in my own strength will always result in failure. However, everything that I do through the strength Christ gives me will always succeed. I must focus my life on giving God the glory in everything I do. Every time I try to do something to improve my lot in life and it fails, I recognize that I tried to do it without Christ being in the forefront.

No matter how tough life gets or how big the problem may seem, with Christ I can proclaim, "I am blessed!" What God has called blessed, no man can curse. No man has the power to curse what God has blessed.

If you listen to the lies of the world around you, being blessed is not what you will feel. You will feel defeated, depressed, and stressed. When you do not feel like you are blessed, you need to start listening to the Word of God.

Negative things will always be coming at us in life. It is one thing to hear the negative voice of the world; it is quite another to accept it and then to act on it. If we want to be a blessing to people, we have to begin to speak as God speaks. When we are in the midst of negative thoughts, we need to speak up and declare God's Word. In order to be able to declare God's Word, we must be a student of the Word of God. We have to read and study in order to be able to confront negativity with what the Lord has said.

The bottom line is what God says about me. Who does God say I am? The Word of God tells me that I am blessed.

Blessed is the man who perseveres under trial, because when he has stood the test, he will receive the crown of life that God has promised to those who love him (James 1:12).

One of the interesting things about this Scripture is that James is teaching us that we are blessed if we endure trials. Who wants to endure trials? Who wants to be blessed? James was encouraging us because he knew we would have trials. Sometimes when you are going through trials and difficulties, your faith is being put to the test. It is in these times that it is good to hear a strong word on endurance.

Not only will you be blessed for what you have gone through, but you will also be blessed for what you are now experiencing if you endure. In a race there may be a first and second runner-up, but there are no prizes for the quitters. If you give up in the midst of the trial and walk away from the faith, you will not receive the prize. However, you will be blessed for making it to the end. Having done all, you must keep on standing.

I am now in school again, and I know that when you take a final examination, it is to your benefit to finish the test. Although you may get some of the questions wrong, the more you answer, the better your chances are of passing the exam. If you leave any answers blank, the question will be marked incorrect. Answering the questions is to your advantage. Stay the course and finish the race.

The day when we receive our eternal blessings and rewards will be a great day. Jesus has promised blessings for those who are faithful. Faithfulness is a matter of attitude. Many times we serve God with conditions, thinking that we will walk with God as long as things are going our way. Faithfulness is serving God without conditions. I will serve God even if things do not go the way I want them to go.

Many times we fail to see how blessed we are because we are out of position. There are many things that move us from a position of blessing, all of which have their root in sin. God requires us to submit to Him if we are to receive His blessings. Please do not allow anything to stand between you and your blessings.

Many times we desire to be blessed, but are we ready? For years my husband prayed the pray of Jabez over me every day.

And Jabez called on the God of Israel saying "Oh, that You would bless me indeed, and enlarge my territory, that Your hand would be with me, and that You would keep me from evil, that I may not cause pain!" So God granted him what he requested (1 Chronicles 4:10 NKJV).

Yes, I wanted to be blessed. However, I was fearful of what "enlarge my territory" meant. I was comfortable where I was and did not want to be stretched too much. My husband kept praying the same prayer over my life, so I knew I might as well come in agreement with what he was praying.

When God enlarges our territory, He wants you to make a greater impact for Him. Territory can mean something different to each of us. In Jabez's cry to God, he was looking at his present circumstances. He knew he was born for more than he was presently experiencing.

I can tell you like Jabez, you were born for more than you are currently doing. My territory was to expand the ministry to women that God had given me. Part of my enlarged territory was to write and publish my first book entitled *Women of Promise*, then to have it republished as an expanded and updated copy titled *Seven Blessing Blockers*. Now I pray the Jabez prayer daily. Enlargement will always produce growing pains, but if you want God to bless you indeed, you have to be willing to allow Him to use you to bring glory to Him. After all, that is why you were created.

In Romans 4:6-8 Paul calls witnesses from the Old Testament to testify about justification through faith. When we receive Christ, we are justified through faith. Our transgressions are forgiven, and the Word of God calls us blessed.

> *David says the same thing when he speaks of the blessedness of the man to whom God credits righteousness apart from works: Blessed are they whose transgressions are forgiven, whose sins are covered. Blessed is the man whose sin the Lord will never count against him* (Romans 4:6-8).

When you accept Jesus Christ as your Savior, you are

blessed. In fact, salvation is the greatest blessing you can receive. With salvation comes so many other blessings—peace, forgiveness, and love, just to name a few.

Now that we agree that we are blessed, the question is, why does God bless us? The obvious reason is that God blesses us so we can be a blessing to others. As we bless others we will continue to be blessed by God.

As God pours His spirit into us, it is our responsibility to share with others the love of Christ. The more we give of ourselves, the more God will bless us. When we give of ourselves to others, God will replenish us with His blessings. I am blessed to be a blessing.

Let us pray.

Dear Lord,

I thank You for Your many blessing in my life. I thank You that You looked beyond my faults and saw the needs in my life. You are a great God, and I appreciate You so much for who You are. I thank You that I am blessed to be a blessing. My prayer today is that You will place someone in my path to whom I can be a blessing. Let me freely give what I have been given, even if it's just a kind word to someone who is hopeless today. In Jesus' name. Amen.

CHAPTER SEVEN

I Am Purpose Driven

Every human being seeks to discover their purpose. What is life without purpose and direction? Many times we stumble through life, hitting and missing, wishing and hoping that maybe we got it right this time. The answers to our frustrations are to discover our purpose. When we know our purpose, life becomes less stressful. Once we have an understanding of not only who we are but whose we are, this revelation will free us to focus on fulfilling our purpose.

In order to be purpose driven we must know the One who selected our purpose. Our heavenly Father, the Creator, knew us before we were conceived in our mother's womb. He was well acquainted with us before the foundation of the world.

According as he hath chosen us in him before the founda-

tion of the world, that we should be holy and without blame before him in love (Ephesians 1:4 KJV).

The fact that God chose me before the foundation of the world was not a coldhearted decision or a fate of doom. It was a decision made out of His great love for me. The love we speak of here is the agape in Greek—the love that is by choice or one's will, not just a sentimental feeling. God made a decision to love us.

You might say, "So what is my purpose? I want to be purpose driven. I do not want to wander aimlessly any longer. I want to accomplish my purpose." If I had a dollar for every time I have heard these words, I would have millions by now.

Many of us want to function within our calling, but we do not know what that calling is. At least that is what we have told ourselves. People spend a lifetime searching for their purpose. Many times our purpose is looking us right in the face, but we do not see it. Many of us will ask, "What is my purpose; why did God put me here?" These are questions that people have asked since the beginning of time.

Why did I ever come forth from the womb to see labor and sorrow, that my days should be consumed with shame? (Jeremiah 20:18)

Before we can know our purpose, we have to know our value. God places great value on us. We are God's most valuable commodity. We are the only ones who can praise Him. In the midst of everything God created, we were created for

His glory. We are so valuable to God that He gave His only Son to die for our sins.

The Scripture teaches in John 3:16,

For God so loved the world that he gave his one and only Son, so that whosoever believes in him shall not perish but have eternal life.

You are valuable to God. The highest value you can put on something is to give your life for it. Jesus did that for us— He gave His life for the world's sins.

When we think that we are unworthy and do not deserve God's love, it causes us to have feelings of self-condemnation. These feelings will cause us to become alienated from Christ. These feeling of alienation and self-condemnation are planted by the enemy. They are meant to steal our joy and to take us off focus. When we begin to focus on other things, we lose sight of the purpose for which we were created.

Your value is not what you have done; your value is not who people say you should be. Your value is based on who God says you are, and God has declared you a person with a purpose. Other people will always want to tell you what you should or should not be doing. But when you know your purpose, you are not easily influenced by them. Scripture teaches us that:

Therefore, there is now no condemnation to those who are in Christ Jesus (Romans 8:1).

It does not matter what we were before Christ; the only

thing that matters is the great value God places on us after we come to Christ. Once we receive Jesus Christ as our personal Savior, the Scripture records that old things are passed away and all things are become new.

Therefore, if anyone is in Christ, he is a new creation; the old has gone, the new has come! (2 Corinthians 5:17).

When God created man, He knew what was ahead for His Son, but He created us anyway. Man's fall in the garden was no surprise to God. He knew what would happen and had already made provision for man's sin. He made a way out for us, but Satan has no way out because he was the originator of sin.

Knowing it would cost the life of His Son, God still did not hesitate to create us. Many times if we know what the outcome will be, we will choose a different path. But because God loved us so much, He could not choose a different path. In God's eyes, we were worth it. Can you imagine that He believed we were worth the life of His Son?

God places a high value on His creation. The love He has for us is as vibrant today as it was in creation. Yes, you are valuable to God. The value He placed on us far exceeded the cost He would have to pay.

So, how do you determine the value of something? You look at how much people are willing to pay for things they really want. Some people pay thousands of dollars for collectible dolls, cars, trains, etc. I remember the Beanie Baby phase. People were going out of their minds trying to collect them, paying ridiculous prices. I would not have paid much for one because they were not worth anything to me.

Now, if it was the Cabbage Patch doll, then that was a different story. I remember standing in line with my sister for hours in a department store for an opportunity to purchase one. After three hours we gave up and went home empty-handed. The dolls we were waiting for were not free. We simply desired an opportunity to make a purchase. Every person who sought a doll that night had to register. Every half hour they would pull a name, and the person selected would have the opportunity to purchase a doll. Those dolls were in high demand, and stores were selling out of them everywhere. People would come in and buy them and go resell them to someone else.

This was the store's way of giving everyone fair access to those dolls. The Cabbage Patch doll period was in the 80s. I remember going home that night very disappointed that I had not been chosen to purchase one. I originally wanted a little girl doll, but when I realized how difficult they were to come by, I would have settled for either gender.

In our current era there are other things we esteem high in value. The Wii Nintendo game has been a hot item for a few years now. Someone called me to see if I could find one for them. People were putting out notices to everyone they knew, trying to locate a Wii. Some people were paying above retail price because they wanted one so badly.

My point is that if you want something badly enough, or

if you place enough value on an item, you will do what you need to do to obtain it. Many are willing to pay above market value just to secure the desired item.

What is your most valuable earthly possession? Is it some property you own, the home you live in, or a classical automobile? As valuable as that material object is to you, would you trade it for the life of one of your children? Absolutely not! There is nothing on this earth worth the life of one of your precious children. Evidently, God thought there was. He thought we were worth enough to redeem us with the life of His one and only Son. You are worth the life of Jesus. This is how valuable God thinks you are worth!

We are so valuable to God because He sees the potential in us. When we discover our purpose and strive to fulfill it, nothing can stop us from succeeding.

For you know that it was not with perishable things such as silver or gold that you were redeemed from the empty way of life handed down to you from your forefathers, but with the precious blood of Christ, a lamb without blemish or defect (1 Peter 1:18-19).

When we consider that Jesus Christ took the world's sins upon Himself as He hung on the cross, we can start to see just how much He thought of us. The way Jesus felt about us, when He hung on the cross, has not changed and never will. God gave His only Son for us. We are worth so much to Him. He paid the price so we do not have to die in our sins. In other words, He paid the debt we owed. Nothing is more valuable to God than His creation. In Deuteronomy 32:10, He calls us the "apple of His eye."

You are valuable to God. When you know your value, you can discover your purpose. God put you here for His purposes, not your purposes; and for His pleasure, not your own pleasure. When you understand that, you will start to see your life from a different perspective.

Isaiah 49:5a says it plainly: *"And now the Lord says —he who formed me n the womb to be his servant."*

We were created for God's glory. We are not here to enjoy ourselves but to enjoy the Lord. We are not here to wander aimlessly through life, working for our own desires. We are here to work for the Lord, for the desires He has for us. Many times we tend to focus on our own desires. We do what we want to do and go where we want to go. We forget that we have a Master and that Master has a master plan for us.

For he chose us in him before the creation of the world to be holy and blameless in his sight (Ephesians 1:4).

God loves us and He wants us to love Him back. God does not **do** love; God **is** love. He created us to worship and to love Him. God's desire for us is that we walk in His will for our lives. That is the purpose for which we were created.

You can ask anyone if God loves them, and the answer probably would be yes. The real question is not does God love you; the question is, do you love Him? When you start to look at purpose, it is not how much God loves us, although He loves us enough to give His Son. The real purpose question is, do I love Him enough to obey His Word? Do I love Him enough to follow His commandments? When we talk about purpose, we have to talk about our love for God.

Many people today are discussing purpose, but what is the benefit of having a purpose driven life? Purpose gives meaning to our lives. Purpose keeps us focused and motivates us. For some of us, we say, "I don't know my purpose." Often I will tell people how to discover the purpose for their life and they will not listen.

How badly do you want to know your purpose? As a young adult in my twenties, I desperately was searching for purpose. I was frustrated because it appeared my purpose was hidden from me. I am convinced now, as a middle-aged woman, that the condition of your heart is the key to discovering your God-ordained purpose.

We are here because God put us here. Our singular most important purpose in life is found in Matthew 22:37, *"Love the Lord your God with all your heart, and with all your soul, and with all your mind."*

When we love God as the Scripture teaches, we will fulfill our purpose. If you want to fulfill your purpose, then everything cannot revolve around you. Every prayer you pray cannot be, "Lord I need this" and "Lord give me that." We have to submit every area of our lives to God.

The focus must not be on us but upon God. When I am seeking to fulfill my purpose, it is no longer about what I want to do, but what God wants me to do. From the deepest and most intimate part of my heart, I am seeking to please God.

It is not enough for us to discover our purpose only. We must walk in purpose. It is time to be purpose driven. Let your purpose motivate you. Many times we let mishaps motivate us. We schedule our lives based on whatever is going on at the moment. A purpose driven person makes a schedule based on what they are trying to achieve. They do not look at life from the perspective of what is happening to them at the moment, but they look at life from the angle of their future destination.

Often we adapt a defeatist attitude from the beginning. We do not understand the authority we have been given. We must learn to speak the Word of God over our own lives. We need to use the power God has given us in His Word.

Put your faith to work. You may not have a clear direction right now. Trust God, have faith, and allow Him to direct your path. Start prophesying over your life to call forth those gifts, callings, and dreams to embrace your purpose. Many times we say, "I know God has called me to do something, but I do not know what it is." If you want to be purpose driven, you have to follow God's plan for your life. If you are not sure of your purpose, pay close attention to the people God places in your life. Why would God give you a gift and not tell you what it is? The Scripture teaches:

"For my thoughts are not your thoughts, neither are your ways my ways," declares the Lord (Isaiah 55:8)**.**

Because we do not think like God, we would never know what He wants us to do unless He told us. As you begin to love God with your whole soul, He will begin to reveal to you His plan. Quite often God will place people around you to help pull your gifts out of you. Pay attention to what people ask from you. What kind of people gravitates toward you? There is a purpose for each person being in your life.

When you are purpose driven, you see everything and everybody as part of your purpose. You will ask questions like: Why is this person in my life? and Who sent this purpose into my life? When you are purpose driven, coincidences do not exist.

I make known the end from the beginning, from ancient times what is still to come. I say, my purpose will stand, and I will do all that I please. From the east I summon a bird of prey, from a far off land a man to fulfill my purpose. What I have said that will I bring about. What I have planned that will I do (Isaiah 46:10-11).

God is faithful to perform His Word. The enemy comes to steal the purpose for which you were created. The devil knows that if he can steal the promise, you will die. The Bible teaches:

"No weapon forged against you will prevail, and you will refute every tongue that accuses you. This is the heritage of the servants of the LORD, and this is their vindication from me," declares the LORD (Isaiah 54:17).

Every believer must purpose in His heart to obey God always. God has given us power over the enemy. He has given us weapons to defend ourselves against the enemy. These weapons are found in the counsel of His Word. Ephesians 6:10-18 teaches us about the armor of God:

> *Be strong in the Lord and in his mighty power. Put on the full armor of God so that you can take your stand against the devil's schemes. For our struggle is not against flesh and blood, but against the rulers, against the authorities, against the powers of this dark world and against the spiritual forces of evil in the heavenly realms. Therefore put on the full armor of God, so that when the day of evil comes, you may be able to stand your ground, and after you have done everything, to stand. Stand firm then, with the belt of truth buckled around your waist, with the breastplate of righteousness in place, and with your feet fitted with the readiness that comes from the gospel of peace. In addition to all this, take up the shield of faith, with which you can extinguish all the flaming arrows of the evil one. Take the helmet of salvation and the sword of the Spirit, which is the word of God. And pray in the Spirit on all occasions with all kinds of prayers and requests. With this in mind, be alert and always keep on praying for all the saints.*

Another weapon God has given us is the clapping of our hands:

> *O clap your hands ye people* (Psalm 47:1).

Shouting hallelujah is also a weapon of my warfare.

> *The seventh time around, when the priests sounded the trumpet blast, Joshua commanded the people, "Shout! For the LORD has given you the city!"* (Joshua 6:16).

When I say the name of Jesus, it is a weapon of my warfare.

And these signs will accompany those who believe: In my name they will drive out demons; they will speak in new tongues; they will pick up snakes with their hands; and when they drink deadly poison, it will not hurt them at all; they will place their hands on sick people, and they will get well (Mark 16: 17-18).

When the enemy is trying to stop you from fulfilling your purpose, use the weapons of your warfare. The enemy does not want you to utilize your weapons of warfare. But it is time for us to stand in the authority we have been given and walk in purpose.

God is carefully ordering the events of your life to accomplish His purpose in your life. God is moving things, changing things, and pushing you into your purpose. Allow the Holy Spirit to direct your every thought and your every step. Do not go ahead of God and do not linger when He says to go.

You are purpose driven; do not be driven by fear. Fear is a strong motivator, but we cannot allow fear to be the main driver in our lives. Many times we are driven by greed or by a need to succeed. Again, these things are definitely motivators. But as we are seeking to please God, we have to be purpose-oriented. Stay focused on God; do not allow disobedience to stop you from fulfilling your purpose.

Let us pray.

Dear Heavenly Father,

I desire to know Your plan and purpose for my life. I commit my life to You now that You will make out of me what You desire me to be. Do not let me go my own way, but keep me in Your way. Even when I desire to go out and do my own thing, I ask that You guide me back to You. I only want to do the things that please You. I want to be found in Your will always. Whatever it takes to keep me focused on Your plan and purpose for my life, I give You permission to do. In Jesus' name. Amen.

CHAPTER EIGHT

I Am Healed

The word *heal* means "to be made sound or whole." To be healed is to have your health restored. This restoration can be spiritual, physical, or mental. To be healed means that everything that was out of alignment has been restored to its proper position. Many people today are out of alignment!

The prayer for healing is the most requested prayer in the church today. Every Sunday that I am blessed with the privilege to minister at the altar, someone comes desiring healing. Some of the requests are for emotional healing but most for physical healing. No one wants to be sick. Everyone wants to be whole again.

I can guarantee you that no one would exchange good health for riches. If the richest person in the world were sick, he or she would give a fortune to be well again. We hear too many stories about people of great wealth seeking alternative health care. They will spend every dime they have to be made whole again.

In Scripture we read many passages that have to do with healing. While doctors and medicine are gifts from God, He is the One that brings the healing. The power of God is greater than any human wisdom.

Now to him who is able to do immeasurably more than all we ask or imagine, according to his power that is at work within us (Ephesians 3:20).

God is able to do more than we can imagine. We do not put our faith in doctors or in medication. God encourages us to call upon Him for healing.

If you listen carefully to the voice of the LORD your God and do what is right in his eyes, if you pay attention to his commands and keep all his decrees, I will not bring on you any of the diseases I brought on the Egyptians, for I am the LORD, who heals you (Exodus 15:26).

We call Him *Jehovah Rapha* because He is the God of healing.

Praise the LORD, O my soul, and forget not all His benefits—who forgives all your sins and heals all your diseases (Psalm 103:2-3).

Many teachers today want us to believe that miracles no longer occur. People who claim to believe God will inform us that miracles were only in the Bible days. They will cite the following Scripture:

Love never fails. But where there are prophecies, they will cease; where there are tongues, they will be stilled; where there is knowledge, it will pass away (1 Corinthians 13:8).

This passage refers to the return of Jesus Christ. When He comes again, we will no longer need prophecies, tongues, and miracles because we will be in His presence. Until then, the anointing, power, and gifts of the Holy Spirit are readily available to help us in every situation!

God's Word reveals how deeply He loves His children and wants us to have health and wholeness.

Whoever does not love does not know God, because God is love. This is how God showed his love among us: He sent his one and only Son into the world that we might live through him (1 John 4:8b-9).

God is love. God showed His love among us by sending His one and only Son into the world that we might live through Him.

The thief comes only to steal and kill and destroy; I have come that they may have life, and have it to the full (John 10:10).

Jesus confirmed what abundant life means for us who choose to believe Him. The Gospels of Matthew, Mark, Luke, and John give several accounts of how Jesus healed people of serious infirmities and illnesses, including blindness, deafness, leprosy, seizures, and paralysis. He even raised dead people to life! Notice the word "all" in the following verse:

When evening came, many who were demon-possessed were brought to him, and he drove out the spirits with a word and healed all the sick (Matthew 8:16).

He healed all the sick. Jesus prepared His disciples to perform the same miracles He performed. The same power that healed in Bible days is working in the lives of believers today.

When Jesus had called the Twelve together, he gave them power and authority to drive out all demons and to cure diseases, and he sent them out to preach the kingdom of God and to heal the sick (Luke 9:1-2).

Jesus gave the disciple power and authority to drive out all evil spirits and to cure all diseases.

I tell you the truth, anyone who has faith in me will do what I have been doing. He will do even greater things than these, because I am going to the Father. And I will do whatever you ask in my name, so that the Son may bring glory to the Father. You may ask me for anything in my name, and I will do it (John 14:12-15).

James 5:14-16 gives very specific instructions about healing:

Is any one of you sick? He should call the elders of the

> *church to pray over him and anoint him with oil in the name of the Lord. And the prayer offered in faith will make the sick person well; the Lord will raise him up. If he has sinned, he will be forgiven. Therefore confess your sins to each other and pray for each other so that you may be healed. The prayer of a righteous man is powerful and effective.*

Scripture serves as a reminder to us that we should forgive others or seek forgiveness before we pray for our healing. If we have sin in our hearts, for example animosity and grudges, our miracles can be blocked.

Psalm 66:18 says, *"If I had cherished sin in my heart, the Lord would not have listened."*

So why are there so many sick people in the world? Sometimes outward physical healing may not occur if the Lord has something else to teach us or accomplish within us. We must be very careful not to judge why others are sick and suffering. In the Scripture below, the disciples felt there must have been sin since the man was blind. Notice what Jesus told them.

> *And his disciples asked him, saying, "Rabbi, who sinned, this man or his parents, that he was born blind?" Jesus answered, "Neither this man nor his parents sinned, but that the works of God should be revealed in him"* (John 9:2-3).

Our duty is simply to ask God in faith for healing, to believe that He is at work, and to trust Him for the outcome.

I Am Healed

Jesus said, "Ask and it will be given to you; seek and you will find; knock and the door will be opened to you" (Matthew 7:7).

In the original Greek, these verbs mean, "Ask and keep on asking; seek and keep on seeking; knock and keep on knocking." We cannot lose hope; we must continue to ask God for healing. Have faith in God.

Now, I am not saying that everyone who is sick brought it on themselves because of choices they made. I worked as a registered nurse for many years in critical care. I have seen suffering up close and personal far too often.

I am also well aware that because of sin in the garden, death came to man. When Adam and Eve made the decision to disobey God, sin entered the world. And the Bible teaches us that death is an appointment for all of us. Sometimes when we do everything we know to do, disease still infects our bodies.

My mission is to call the body of Christ into accountability. We cannot abuse our bodies and anticipate a good outcome. We must take care of the bodies that God has given us so they will serve us for a long time.

Knowing what the Word of God says and with the frequent request for physical healing, I have to ask myself why there so many sick people in our world, and more importantly, in our church?

I do believe that a majority of sickness today is due to our lifestyle. We make poor choices concerning what we put in our bodies. Many of us do not exercise regularly. Some of us even continue our bad habits of smoking, drinking, not getting enough sleep, and negative thinking. In spite of these bad judgment calls, we continue to ask God for healing.

We say one thing with our mouths, but our actions are saying another. Our mouths are saying, "I want to be made whole. I want to have my health restored." But our actions are saying, "Let me continue in my current life choices."

> *What? know ye not that your body is the temple of the Holy Ghost which is in you, which ye have of God, and ye are not your own? For ye are bought with a price: therefore glorify God in your body, and in your spirit, which are God's* (1 Corinthians 6:19-20 KJV).

Even though this Scripture deals with sexual sin, I believe we can apply it to the sins we commit by putting things in our bodies that should not be ingested. Paul is teaching the Corinthians that sexual sin is done against the body, not outside of it. Paul exhorts the Corinthians to flee any attraction to indulge in sexual sin. He teaches them that they—like us—are purchased with the death of Jesus Christ. The cost He paid was to redeem us from sin, back to the Father.

It is ironic that Jesus gave His life for our freedom, and we in turn destroy our lives by neglecting our health. We have to wake up; the devil wants to kill us anyway he can. Many of us would not think of using drugs or alcohol. However, we put poison in our system three times a day at mealtime.

Heart disease is still the number one killer of women. We know what causes heart disease. Some things we can change and some things we cannot change. What can I do to protect myself? For both men and women, the biggest factors that contribute to heart disease are smoking, high blood pressure, high cholesterol, family history, and age.

Take a moment to look at your lifestyle, family history, and your general health. There is nothing you can do about your family history or your age. But we can make lifestyle changes to avoid many of the other risk factors.

Smoking is a major risk factor for heart disease in women. A large percentage of heart attacks in women under the age of fifty are related to smoking. Some of the medical reports that I have read suggest that if you stop smoking, you can lower your risk of heart attack by one third within two years. Women who smoke and use birth control pills increase their risk even more, especially if birth control pill usage continues after age thirty-five.

Breathing smoke from someone else's cigarettes can be equally as bad for your heart and lungs. If you live with someone who smokes, encourage them to quit. A nurse I worked with many years ago died from lung cancer. She had the form of lung cancer that is directly related to cigarette smoking. The strange thing was she had never smoked a day in her life, but her husband was a smoker.

Treating high blood pressure can lower your risk of heart attack and stroke. That is where that healthy eating comes into play. Losing weight, exercising regularly, and eating a healthy diet are all ways to help control high blood pressure. Reducing how much salt you consume can also help.

Control your cholesterol level. This is a challenge for many of us because high cholesterol runs in our families. Diet is a key part of lowering high cholesterol levels. I believe that we need to do our part in staying healthy.

When we have done everything we know to do, we can go to our God. My point is to stop having the pastor lay hands on you because the doctor said you have high cholesterol unless you are willing to make the necessary changes. Prayer and "trans fat" do not work very well together.

Maintain a healthy weight. Extra weight puts strain on your heart and arteries. Exercise and a low-fat diet can help you lose weight. Being overweight means you have a higher risk for many other health problems, especially diabetes, high blood pressure, and heart disease.

Regular exercise is both mentally and physically rewarding. Remember, your heart is a muscle. It needs regular exercise to stay in shape. Aerobic exercise, such as walking, swimming, jogging, or biking, gives your heart the best workout. You can also use fitness equipment like exercise bicycles, treadmills, and ski machines when exercising indoors. Finding a partner may make exercise more enjoyable for you. If you enjoy it, you are more likely to be consistent at it.

Eat a low-fat diet. Keep fat calories to 30 percent or less of the total calories you eat during a day and avoid saturated fat. I will let my sister the nutritionist write a healthy eating book, but I want to inform the people of God that we are killing ourselves slowly. We are healed! God has already healed us. We have to perform as healed people. We have to act like we are healed and eat like we are healed.

People of God, let me show you something. If I told you, "You are a millionaire," you would start acting like a millionaire. If you were a good steward, you would begin to position yourself, putting safeguards in place to protect your fortune. If I told you, "You are broke; you lost your fortune." You would not go out racking up debt; you would immediately change your lifestyle. We are healed, so let's start to live like we are healed. Let's position ourselves to safeguard our health.

> *Do not be deceived, God is not mocked; for whatever a man sows, that he will also reap. For he who sows to his flesh will of the flesh reap corruption, but he who sows to the Spirit will of the Spirit reap everlasting life. And let us not grow weary while doing good, for in due season we shall reap if we do not lose heart* (Galatians 6:7-8).

The principle of sowing and reaping is noted in this text. Many times we think that we can mock God by sowing to our flesh, thinking we will escape the harvest of destruction. We cannot defy principles and expect to receive God's blessing.

When farmers plant seeds, they do not produce an immediate harvest. It takes time for the seeds to grow. What you

Identity Crisis

put in your body today will not produce today. It may take many years for the affects to show.

In the growth process of the planted seed, several things can be done to impede the development of a harvest. For example, if the seed is not watered properly, it will not grow. In other words, we can do several things to change the course of our health. If you have been putting unhealthy foods in your body for a number of years, you can stop today. You will not necessarily see the affect of the change today, but in due season you will reap the benefits of a healthy lifestyle.

The principle we see working is that what we are today is due to what we did yesterday. And what we do today will determine what we become tomorrow. Pledge to walk in healing today by guarding your health. We are healed!

Let us pray.

Dear Heavenly Father,

Your Word declares that You are the God who heals all our diseases. I thank You for Your healing power operating in my life. I take authority now over sickness in my body, and I stand on Your Word that I am healed. Please grant me wisdom to change the things I can in my life. Help me commit myself to healthy eating and regular exercise. I dedicate my body as a temple to You today. I want to give You the best of me. I thank You in Jesus' name. Amen.

CHAPTER NINE

I Am Loved

In 1 Corinthians 13:1-13 we see a vivid description of what love is and what love is not.

> *If I speak in the tongues of men and of angels, but have not love, I am only a resounding gong or a clanging cymbal. If I have the gift of prophecy and can fathom all mysteries and all knowledge, and if I have a faith that can move mountains, but have not love, I am nothing. If I give all I possess to the poor and surrender my body to the flames but have not love, I gain nothing. Love is patient, love is kind. It does not envy, it does not boast, it is not proud. It is not rude, it is not self-seeking, it is not easily angered, it keeps no record of wrongs. Love does not delight in evil but rejoices with the truth. It always protects, always trusts, always hopes, always perseveres. Love never fails. But where there are prophecies, they will cease;*

where there are tongues, they will be stilled; where there is knowledge, it will pass away. For we know in part and we prophesy in part, but when perfection comes, the imperfect disappears. When I was a child, I talked like a child, I thought like a child, I reasoned like a child. When I became a man, I put childish ways behind me. Now we see but a poor reflection as in a mirror; then we shall see face to face. Now I know in part; then I shall know fully, even as I am fully known. And now these three remain: faith, hope and love. But the greatest of these is love.

Many times we search for a true description of love. God's Word above is very clear on how love demonstrates itself.

The words "charity" and "love" is derived from the word *agape*, that self-giving divine love which radiates from God and is to be seen reflected in believers. It is the love that is concerned for others rather than self.

The New Testament was written in Greek, a rich language that has four different words that describe four differ types of love. The first word is one of affection. It is the love for family. This word describes the love that members of the animal kingdom have for their offspring. This word is most often used in referring to the love that parents have for their children. As special as the love of a parent is, this is not the love expressed in the above Scripture.

Another word that never appears in the Greek New Testament is the word from which we get our English word

Identity Crisis

"erotic." This is the word that describes the love of attraction between the two sexes. Although marriage is very important to God, it is not that love we see in this scripture.

Philadelphia is called "the city of brotherly love." The very word comes to us from another Greek word, often used in Scripture that refers to friendship. This love is also very special, but it is not the lasting love portrayed in the verses above. Brotherly love is long lasting, but it is often based on mutual affection. Friends are people who have common interests and enjoy spending time with each other.

Everyone wants to be loved. We search high and low looking for love. The sad thing is that we look in all of the wrong places. When we seek love outside of God's will, we are disappointed. Many times we anticipate one thing but receive another.

I have heard wives say many times, "He wasn't like this when I met him." I think he probably was, and you chose not to see it. People do not change that much. We see what we want to see and ignore what we do not want to see. Denial is a place of comfort for many people. Often we think, "If I do not say it, then it is not real.

Most, if not all, of the annoying habit that display themselves in marriage were present prior to marriage. We overlook things because we think, *Oh, he will change*. In some cases we say to ourselves, "I caused him to act like that, so I will change."

Love is a universal language. I have read studies of

I Am Loved

Alzheimer patients who can no longer recognize loved ones. Even though they cannot recognize the loved one, they are able to recognize love. One story I heard was about a father with Alzheimer's disease who said to his daughter, "I do not know who you are, but I know you love me." True love can be felt for love is an action word. When you love someone, you show them and do not just tell them, "I love you."

God showed us how much He loved us, by giving His only begotten Son to die for us. The Scripture records that there is no greater demonstration of love.

My command is this: Love each other as I have loved you. Greater love has no one than this that he lay down his life for his friends. You are my friends if you do what I command (John 15:12-14).

The Word of God is filled with demonstrations of God's love for us. He tells us over and over in Scripture just how much He loves us. The Greek language in which the New Testament was written uses several words translated "love."

Phileo (verb) means "to have ardent affection and feeling—a type of impulsive love" (*Nelson's New Illustrated Bible Dictionary*, 1995, Love). This love is the ordinary, human type of love and fondness that we have for a friend and is frequently defined as "brotherly love." In John 21:15-16, Jesus asked Peter if he loved Him with the *agapao* type of love, and Peter answered that he had the normal human *phileo* type of love for Him. Later, after receiving the Holy Spirit, Peter would be able to fully demonstrate *agapao*-type of godly love, serving others throughout his lifetime.

When they had finished eating, Jesus said to Simon Peter, "Simon son of John, do you truly love me more than these?"

"Yes, Lord," he said, "you know that I love you." Jesus said, "Feed my lambs."

Again Jesus said, "Simon son of John, do you truly love me?"

He answered, "Yes, Lord, you know that I love you." Jesus said, "Take care of my sheep."

Eros (noun) refers to sexual, erotic love or desire. True love, as explained in the Bible, never focuses on oneself and one's feelings or emotions, but is instead *outwardly focused on others*—wanting to best serve and care for them. True love is beautifully described in the opening Scripture in 1 Corinthians 13.

Storge means family affection. This word refers to the love of a parent to a child and a child to the parent. Storge talks about family affection between family members. There is a certain sense of family affection that you have one for another because you are of the same family. Family ties run deep unless something comes in between. In our society today, family affection is not as strong as it should be. Many times family members are at war against each other. But normally family affection runs strong with those of the same kin. "Blood is thicker than water." That kind of family affection is the word storge.

This type of love also refers to the intuitive bond between animals and their young. We see in the animal kingdom how the mother protects her young. It is very fascinating to watch the Discovery Channel and see how the black mother bear protects her cubs.

The love that God has for us is called *agape*, unconditional love.

For God so loved the world that he gave his one and only Son, that whoever believes in him shall not perish but have eternal life (John 3:16).

Agapao (verb, noun form, *agape*) is a special word representing the divine love of God toward His Son, humanity in general, and believers. The word agapao is also used to portray the outwardly focused love that God expects us as believers to have for one another. This is a special type of Christian love, "whether exercised toward the brethren, or toward men generally, is not an impulse from the feelings, it does not always run with the natural inclinations, nor does it spend itself only upon those for whom some affinity is discovered" (*Vine's Complete Expository Dictionary of Old and New Testament Words*, Love).

The Bible notes that human marriage is modeled after the divine relationship between Christ and the Church. For this reason husbands are instructed in the Word of God to love their wives with this kind of outgoing, selfless love.

Husbands, love your wives, just as Christ loved the church and gave himself up for her. For this reason a man will leave his father and mother and be united to his wife, and the two will become one flesh. This is a profound mystery—but I am talking about Christ and the church (Ephesians 5:25, 31-32).

Agape is the kind of love expressed in John 15:13 as "greater love." There is no greater love than the kind of love that would cause someone to lay down their life for a friend. Jesus Himself perfectly exemplified this kind of love throughout His lifetime, continually giving of Himself and His time and energies to serve others. The ultimate demonstration of His love was when He gave His life as a sacrifice for all of humanity. This is the kind of love God wants each of us to epitomize in our lives and above all in our marriages.

Agape love embraces the intellect as well as the emotions. Agape love is a decision of the will that says, "By the power of the Holy Spirit living and working in me, I choose to love this way." Agape love always gives, never expecting anything in return. Agape is not based on any mutual attraction for the object of its affection. It is love that loves the unlovable, love that loves those that may by all outward appearances be unattractive indeed. Agape love knows no limits; it sets no boundaries.

When we love agape style, we always look out for the well-being of those we love, placing their interests before our own. Agape love follows in the footsteps of Jesus. He always sets the example for us by practicing what He preaches, for as they drove the nails through His hands and feet He prayed,

Father, forgive them; for they do not know what they are doing (Luke 23:34).

Agape love is the self sacrificial love of Jesus who left His heavenly throne to die on the cross for us when we were at our worst, when we were most unlovable. The love Jesus has for us is not dependent on how we behave. His love is something on which we can always depend.

For God so loved—words cannot illustrate how much God loved us. He had to show us. He showed us by giving His Son. The Son in return gave His life to redeem us back to the Father. Christ's death on the cross was the act of God's immense love for us.

Everyone deserves to be loved. Many of us struggle with the concept of love. Relationship after relationship ends, and we continue to search for love. Oftentimes when a relationship ends, we start to doubt ourselves and wonder, "What is wrong with me?" Rejection is always difficult. But we cannot allow others to make us feel bad about who we are.

When we search for love and come up empty-handed, we might think, "Why can't I find love?" The answer is that we are looking in all the wrong places for love. We deserve to be loved, but we can also give love. Everyone deserves to be loved, and in return, we should offer love. The love we offer each other does not have to be romantic love. We can offer the same love that Christ offers to us daily in His Word.

Many times the love we experience from others is fleeting. People quite often will love you when you do what they want you to do. If you deviate from the normal, their love in some case is withdrawn. It does not matter how hard we try, ultimately we will fail people. We must know that we are loved by God and that His love is unconditional. There is nothing we can do to disappoint God. He knows everything there is to know about us, and He still loves us.

I know I am loved by God, regardless of who else loves me or does not love me. I can always depend on my heavenly Father to love me unconditionally. I am loved and so are you.

I Am Loved

Let us pray.

Dear Heavenly Father,

I thank You for Your unconditional love. You gave the ultimate sacrifice when You died on the cross for my sins. I thank You that Your love never fails. Your love is not dependent on me nor on how I behave, but Your love is true. Many have said they loved me in the past, but they have rejected me. I thank You, Father, that Your love comforts me when I am hurting. Your love gives me joy in those times of despair. I have never known a love as great as Yours. Thank You for loving me. In Jesus' name I pray. Amen.

CHAPTER TEN

My True Identity

You might be saying, "So God says I am beautiful, prosperous, blessed, purpose driven, healed, loved, and the righteousness of God, but I do not feel like I am." Your true identity is not based on how you feel. There are days I do not feel like being a wife, mother, teacher, pastor, student, or anything else. The fact that I do not feel like it does not change who I am.

Some days I feel like pulling the covers over my head and staying in bed. I do not have a desire to be anything to anyone on that day. I just want to be left alone. Friend, when I feel like this, let me tell you what I do. I reach deep inside and pull on the Word of God that lives in my heart. I begin to boldly declare God's Word over my life.

Even when we do not feel like it, we need to continue to

press on and walk in divine purpose on a daily basis. How do you do this? You do it by applying the truth of God's Word to your heart. We must learn to lean and depend on God.

Thing will change from time to time, but God will not change. Neither does He change His mind. He loved you while you were in your sins and He still loves you today. Jesus came to earth with the purpose of redeeming us back to the Father. It does not matter how bad you think you have been, you are still loved by God.

You are created by a loving Creator who uniquely designed you for His glory. We were created to worship our Creator. Our true joy comes when we are fulfilling our purpose. Your relationship with God is the single most important relationship you will ever have.

I see many lonely people in this world—people who love God yet feel lonely. When we connect in relationship with our Creator, things will change. We are created with a longing within us that can only be filled by returning to the Father.

We search for many things to fill the emptiness, but nothing works. Many times we try drugs, alcohol, sex, money, work, and sometimes we even try working in ministry. Only a relationship with God will fill the longing of our hearts.

Knowing who we are in Christ and walking in that truth is so fulfilling. So how do we discover our true identity? When I want to see what I look like, I take a look in the mirror. When you want to know your true identity, take a look in the mirror. The mirror that I am speaking of is God's Word. When we look in the Word of God we see ourselves. We see what we are doing right and what we are doing wrong.

When we look in a natural mirror and see something wrong with us, what do we do? We certainly do not walk away from the mirror without changing something if we can. So when I turn to God's Word, I ask my Creator, "Who am I? Who did You create me to be?" Perhaps, I am not living the way I should, so I look in the mirror—Word of God—to see what changes need to be made. God's Word will tell me exactly who I am. When I read the Word of God, I open my ears to listen. I want to hear what God says about me. I want to know who He says I am.

I want to share a few Scriptures with you that tell you who God said you are.

I have been made one with all who are in Christ Jesus.
There is neither Jew nor Greek, there is neither slave nor free man, there is neither male nor female; for you are all one in Christ Jesus (Galatians 3:28).

I am a friend of God.
No longer do I call you slaves, for the slave does not know what his master is doing; but I have called you friends, for all things that I have heard from My Father I have made known to you (John 15:15).

I am a child of God.
But as many as received Him, to them He gave the right

My True Identity

to become children of God, even to those who believe in His name (John 1:12).

As a child of God, I am a fellow heir with Christ.
Now if we are children, then we are heirs—heirs of God and co-heirs with Christ, if indeed we share in his sufferings in order that we may also share in his glory (Romans 8:17).

My body is a temple of the Holy Spirit who dwells in me.
Don't you know that you yourselves are God's temple and that God's Spirit lives in you? (1 Corinthians 3:16).

Do you not know that your body is a temple of the Holy Spirit, who is in you, whom you have received from God? You are not your own (1 Corinthians 6:19).

I am a new creature in Christ.
Therefore, if anyone is in Christ, he is a new creation; the old has gone, the new has come! (2 Corinthians 5:17).

I am chosen, holy, and blameless before God.
For he chose us in him before the creation of the world to be holy and blameless in his sight. In love (Ephesians 1:4).

I am God's workmanship created to produce good works.
For we are God's workmanship, created in Christ Jesus to do good works, which God prepared in advance for us to do (Ephesians 2:10).

I am a member of Christ's body and a partaker of His promise.
This mystery is that through the gospel the Gentiles are heirs together with Israel, members together of one body, and sharers together in the promise in Christ Jesus (Ephesians 3:6).

For we are members of his body (Ephesians 5:30).

I am light in the Lord.
For you were once darkness, but now you are light in the Lord. Live as children of light (Ephesians 5:8).

I am a citizen of heaven.
But our citizenship is in heaven. And we eagerly await a Savior from there, the Lord Jesus Christ (Philippians 3:20).

I have been made complete in Christ.
And you have been given fullness in Christ, who is the head over every power and authority (Colossians 2:10).

There are many more scriptures that speak of our true identity, and I encourage you to explore God's Word. As you do, you will see God has many compliments for you. He has uniquely designed you according to His purpose and His plan. You are indeed special to Him. No one can do what God created you to do. God created us, and He loves us so much, He sent His Son Jesus to die for us and pay for our sins so we can be made perfect.

My True Identity

Only you can fulfill the plan of God for your life. He created you and me. He made the earth for us and He made us for His pleasure. You are not a mistake nor an accident. God made us in His image. When I read God's Word and all the wonderful things He says about me, I am reassured that He knows me intimately.

I am a child of the Most High. I am treasured by God. He chose my design, and He made me as He did for a reason. God wanted me to be just who I am. He made me to represent Him. When one invites Jesus Christ to live in his heart, one can boldly proclaim "I am who God created me to be."

Many times we have problems with our self-image or self-esteem because we do not know who we are. I am wonderfully made by God.

The reason I stand perfectly clean and pure before Him is found in His Word.

God made him who had no sin to be sin for us, so that in him we might become the righteousness of God (2 Corinthians 5:21).

His Word also says that I am so loved by Him (John 3:16). Is there anyone that you love enough to give your life for? Is there anyone you love enough to give the life of one of your children for? I could see giving my life for someone I loved, but I do not know anyone I love enough to give the life of one of my children for.

Identity Crisis

It is vital that we seek God for our true identity. We can not look to others to affirm us. Many times wives look to their husband for affirmation. Yes, the husband should be able to validate his wife. But what happens when he is not up to the challenge? We must look to our heavenly Father for affirmation; He is always up to the challenge.

I can always go to God when I want to know who I really am; I do not ask the opinions of those around me. I ask my heavenly Father, the One who created me. Only He knows my true identity. Others will judge me by what they see. My identity might change from day to day in the eyes of others. It depends on how the person feels, what kind of night they had, etc. People change like the weather. Many will love you today and hate you tomorrow.

As a pastor, many times I have people come into my life. Some say God sent them to be a blessing and a help to me. They say things such as, "God told me that I am supposed to help you." Or "God placed me in your life to be a blessing to you." Some of you reading this know what I am talking about. It is always interesting to me how if God told them that, then does it mean God changed His mind when they leave? Am I no longer worthy of their help, or do I no longer need to be blessed?

Thank God, He is faithful to stay with us. He said in His Word that He would never leave us. Even if we do things to disappoint Him, He is faithful to remain with us. I love knowing that God is always going to be with me. I will always be His beloved child. Thank God for His mercy and His grace, always present.

My True Identity

As Christians we need to remain focused on God. If we look at the economic conditions in the world, we can be sidetracked. If I looked at my bank account, it might not look so good. The absences of funds would lead me to believe that I am broke. But when I look at God's Word and I see that my Father is rich in houses and land, I know that no matter what my bank account looks like, I am confident that my God will supply my needs.

If I looked at the doctor's report, I might start to believe that I am sick. When I look at God's Word, I see that I am healed of all my diseases. So instead of calling myself sick, I call myself healed in Jesus' name.

Things are not always what they look like. We have to separate fact from truth. The facts may say one thing, but the truth of God's Word may say something differently. I know as long as I stand on the Word of God, I will not fail. The facts are that right now as I write this book, my husband has been diagnosed with cancer. The facts are that neither one of us have worked in the past eight months. The facts are that he has been out of the pulpit for a few months. The facts are that our ministry is suffering. People are exiting and the finances are low. In addition to my husband's illness, my mother is suffering from cancer and is very ill.

If I want to dwell on the facts, I could fill these pages with many facts of my life, but I prefer to fill the pages with truth. The truth is, what does God's Word say about our lives and our situations? I thank God for the manifestation of His Word in our lives. Things are not always what they appear to be. Listen to what God has to say.

Identity Crisis

By the world's yardstick, we do not measure much. Thank God we do not rely on the world to tell us who we are. When we look at the truth, we should see who God says we are. We are whole, walking in abundance. We are doing battle in the spiritual realm, bringing souls to the Lord. We have overflow in our ministry and the church is fulfilling its purpose.

Yes, I know you might be confused about your identity. My friend, never forget who God says you are. Always remember that you are more than a conqueror through Christ Jesus.

*No, in all these things we are more than **conquerors** through him who loved us* (Romans 8:37, emphasis added**).**

Remember that if God be for you, then who can be against you?

*What, then, shall we say in response to this? If God is for us, who can be **against** us?* (Romans 8:31, emphasis added**).**

As we seek to discover our true identity, let us always remember to ask the Creator. God does not lie; He will tell us our true identity.

God is not a man, that he should lie, nor a son of man, that he should change his mind. Does he speak and then not act? Does he promise and not fulfill? **(**Numbers 23:19**).**

Let us pray.

Dear Heavenly Father,

I thank you that You are God. Even when we go through times of distress, You are right there with us. I know You love me and that You created me for Your glory. I ask now, Lord Jesus, that You would help me to stand on the truth of Your Word. No matter what comes or what goes, I want to remain focused on You and Your purpose for my life. I speak healing and wholeness now over the lives of those who are in need. You have a plan and a purpose for our lives. Please order my steps in Your Word. It is my sincere desire to fulfill Your plan and purpose for my life. Keep me abiding in Your Word for Your Word is true. These things I humbly ask in Jesus' name. Amen.

Meet the Author

Evelyn Johnson-Taylor was called by God to minister and teach women from all walks of life. Pastor Evelyn's heart is for their spiritual growth and development, and she has dedicated her life to encouraging them. She is the founder of Women of Promise, a ministry designed to address the obstacles that stand between women and their ability to reap the promises of God's Word.

Evelyn worked as a registered nurse in critical care for fifteen years. She has a Bachelors Degree in Women's Studies, a Masters Degree in Ministry, and with God's help will complete her doctoral work this year.

She serves as Co-pastor of Good News Global Ministries in Tampa, Florida. Her husband, Bishop Scott Taylor, is the Senior Pastor and overseer of Good News Global Ministries Inc. Evelyn speaks, teaches, and preaches about issues that pertain to women.

The Taylors have been married and in ministry together for more than eighteen years and are the proud parents of two daughters.

Pastor Evelyn is available as a conference teacher or speaker. She is also available as a mentor, life coach or spiritual counselor. Please visit her website at www.evelynjtaylor.org or email her at: evelynjtaylor@aol.com.

www.ingramcontent.com/pod-product-compliance
Lightning Source LLC
Chambersburg PA
CBHW071929290426
44110CB00013B/1540